BE A BETTER PROJECT MANAGER

Published by:
Lotus Press : Publishers & Distributors

BE A BETTER PROJECT MANAGER

B.K. Pathak

Lotus PRESS

4735/22, Prakash Deep Building
Ansari Road, Darya Ganj,
New Delhi-110002

Lotus Press : Publishers & Distributors
Unit No. 220, 2nd Floor, 4735/22, Prakash Deep Building,
Ansari Road, Darya Ganj, New Delhi- 110002
Ph.: 32903912, 23280047 • E-mail : lotus_press@sify.com
www.lotuspress.co.in

Be a Better Project Manager

ISBN: 978-81-8382-277-0

Published by : **Lotus Press : Publishers & Distributors** New Delhi-110002
Printed at : Concept Imprint, Delhi

PREFACE

Projects are finite in length, usually one-time pieces of work involving a number of activities that must be completed within a given time frame, and on a fixed budget. Projects that are more complex need a great deal of planning, and benefit from a formal, disciplined management approach. For this reason, there is a requirement of project manager.

Managing projects well requires a great deal of time, skill, and finance. Project managers are expected to take an uncertain event and make a certain promise to deliver. They are also expected to do this within a specified time and within a limited budget.

If you are looking for a more robust approach to project management then this book a perfect resource for you. It not only guides you through the traditional methods, but also covers the adaptive and extreme approaches as well. It is a fast track guide to becoming a competent and better project manager.

B. K. Pathak

CONTENTS

1

RESPONSIBILITIES OF A PROJECT MANAGER

A project manager is the person responsible for accomplishing the stated project objectives. Key project manager's responsibilities include creating clear and attainable project objectives, building the project requirements, and managing the triple constraint for projects, which are cost, time, and quality.

A project manager is often a client representative and has to determine and implement the exact needs of the client, based on knowledge of the firm they are representing. The ability to adapt to the various internal procedures of the contracting party, and to form close links with the nominated representatives, is essential in ensuring that the key issues of cost, time, quality and above all, client satisfaction, can be realized.

The term 'project manager' has come to be used generically to describe anyone given responsibility to complete a project. However, it is more properly used to describe a person with full responsibility and the same level of authority required to complete a project. If a person does not have high levels of both responsibility and authority then they are better described as a project administrator, coordinator, facilitator or expeditor.

RESPONSIBILITIES OF THE PROJECT MANAGER

The specific responsibilities of the project manager vary depending on the industry, the company size, the company maturity, and the company culture. However, there are some responsibilities that are common to all project managers, noting:

- Developing the project plan
- Managing the project stakeholders
- Managing the project team
- Managing the project risk
- Managing the project schedule
- Managing the project budget
- Managing the project conflicts

Anyone who has ever worked on a project will agree that making a project succeed is no simple task. The difficulties manifest themselves in (extreme) delays, (extreme) budget over-runs, inadequate results, dissatisfied customers, high stress among the project team and other undesirable outcomes. What is the cause of all of these problems?

Projects are characterised by four features: a group of people, a goal, limited time and money and a certain level of uncertainty regarding whether the goals will be achieved. Project managers are involved with all of these aspects. Supervising and directing a project is thus anything but an easy task.

Projects are becoming increasingly common. Project-based working methods have also found their way into non-profit organizations. The rules of the game for projects in non-profit organizations differ from those in commercial organizations. Political factors play a particularly important role in non-profit organizations. This makes it even more difficult for projects to succeed, compared to projects in which commercial aspects play a part. Project leaders should be aware of this and be able to play the game of politics.

UNDERSTANDING THE PROJECT PHASES

Dividing a project into phases makes it possible to lead it in the best possible direction. Through this organization into phases, the total work load of a project is divided into smaller components, thus making it easier to monitor. The following paragraphs describe a phasing model that has been useful in practice. It includes six phases:

- Initiation phase
- Definition phase
- Design phase
- Development phase
- Implementation phase
- Follow-up phase

Initiation Phase

The initiation phase is the beginning of the project. In this phase, the idea for the project is explored and elaborated. The goal of this phase is to examine the feasibility of the project. In addition, decisions are made concerning who is to carry out the project, which party (or parties) will be involved and whether the project has an adequate base of support among those who are involved.

In this phase, the current or prospective project leader writes a proposal, which contains a description of the above-mentioned matters. Examples of this type of project proposal include business plans and grant applications. The prospective sponsors of the project evaluate the proposal and, upon approval, provide the necessary financing. The project officially begins at the time of approval.

Questions to be answered in the initiation phase include the following:

- Why this project?
- Is it feasible?
- Who are possible partners in this project?
- What should the results be?
- What are the boundaries of this project?

The ability to say 'no' is an important quality in a project manager. Projects tend to expand once people have become excited about them. Projects to which people keep adding objectives and projects that keep expanding are nearly certain to go off schedule, and they are unlikely to achieve their original goals.

In the initiation phase, the project partners enter a (temporary) relationship with each other. To prevent the development of false expectations concerning the results of the project, it makes sense to explicitly agree on the type of project that is being started:

- a research and development project;
- a project that will deliver a prototype or 'proof of concept';
- a project that will deliver a working product.

The choice for a particular type of project largely determines its results. For example, a research and development project delivers a report that examines the technological feasibility of an application. A project in which a prototype is developed delivers all of the functionalities of an application, but they need not be suitable for use in a particular context. A project that delivers a working product must also consider matters of maintenance, instructions and the operational management of the application.

Many misunderstandings and conflicts arise because the parties that are involved in a project are not clear on these matters. Customers may expect a working product, while the members of the project team think they are developing a prototype. A sponsor may think that the project will produce a working piece of software, while the members of the project team must first examine whether the idea itself is technically feasible.

Definition Phase

After the project plan has been approved, the project enters the second phase: the definition phase. In this phase, the requirements that are associated with a project result are specified as clearly as possible. This involves identifying the expectations that all of the involved parties have with regard to the project result. How many files are to be archived? Should the metadata conform to the Data Documentation Initiative format, or will the Dublin Core (DC) format suffice? May files be deposited in their original format, or will only those that conform to the Preferred Standards be accepted? Must the depositor of a dataset ensure that it has been processed adequately in the archive, or is this the responsibility of the archivist? Which guarantees will be made on the results of the project? The list of questions goes on and on.

It is important to identify the requirements as early in the process as possible. There are several categories of project requirements that can serve as a memory aid:

- Preconditions
- Functional requirements
- Operational requirements
- Design limitations

Preconditions form the context within which the project must be conducted. Examples include legislation, working-condition regulations and approval requirements. These requirements cannot be influenced from within the project. Functional requirements are requirements that have to do with the quality of the project result. Operational requirements involve the use of the project result. For example, after a software project has been realised, the number of malfunctions that occur must be reduced by ninety per cent. Finally, design limitations are requirements that involve the actual realisation of the project. For example, the project cannot involve the use of toxic materials or international partners for whom it is unclear whether they use child labour.

Design Phase

The list of requirements that is developed in the definition phase can be used to make design choices. In the design phase, one or more designs are developed, with which the project result can apparently be achieved. Depending on the subject of the project, the products of the design phase can include dioramas, sketches, flow charts, site trees, HTML screen designs, prototypes, photo impressions and UML schemas. The project supervisors use these designs to choose the definitive design that will be produced in the project. This is followed by the development phase. As in the definition phase, once the design has been chosen, it cannot be changed in a later stage of the project.

In a young, very informal company, the design department was run by an artist. The term 'design department' was not accurate in this case; it was more a group of designers who were working together. In addition, everyone was much too busy, including the head of the department.

One project involved producing a number of designs, which were quite important to the success of the project.

A young designer on the project team created the designs. Although the head of the design department had ultimate responsibility for the designs, he never attended the meetings of the project team when the designs were to be discussed. The project leader always invited him, and sent him e-mails containing his young colleague's sketches, but the e-mails remained unanswered. The project leader and the young designer erroneously assumed that the department head had approved the designs. The implementation phase began. When the project was nearly finished, the result was presented to the department head, who became furious and demanded that it be completely redone. The budget, however, was almost exhausted.

Development Phase

During the development phase, everything that will be needed to implement the project is arranged. Potential suppliers or subcontractors are brought in, a schedule is made, materials and tools are ordered, instructions are given to the personnel and so forth. The development phase is complete when implementation is ready to start. All matters must be clear for the parties that will carry out the implementation.

In some projects, particularly smaller ones, a formal development phase is probably not necessary. The important point is that it must be clear what must be done in the implementation phase, by whom and when.

Implementation Phase

The project takes shape during the implementation phase. This phase involves the construction of the actual project result. Programmers are occupied with encoding, designers are involved in developing graphic material, contractors are building, the actual reorganisation takes place. It is during this phase that the project becomes visible to outsiders, to whom it may appear that the project has just begun. The implementation phase is the 'doing' phase, and it is important to maintain the momentum.

In one project, it had escaped the project team's attention that one of the most important team members was expecting to become a father at any moment and would thereafter be completely unavailable for about a month. When the time came, an external specialist was brought in to take over his work, in order to keep the team from grinding to a halt. Although the team was able to proceed, the external expertise put a considerable dent in the budget.

At the end of the implementation phase, the result is evaluated according to the list of requirements that was created in the definition phase. It is also evaluated according to the designs. For example, tests may be conducted to determine whether the web application does indeed support Explorer 5 and Firefox 1.0 and higher. It may be determined whether the trim on the building has been made according to the agreement, or whether the materials that were used were indeed those that had been specified in the definition phase. This phase is complete when all of the requirements have been met and when the result corresponds to the design.

Those who are involved in a project should keep in mind that it is hardly ever possible to achieve a project result that precisely meets all of the requirements that were originally specified in the definition phase. Unexpected events or advancing insight sometimes require a project team to deviate from the original list of requirements or other design documents during the implementation of the project. This is a potential source of conflict, particularly if an external customer has ordered the project result. In such cases, the customer can appeal to the agreements that were made during the definition phase.

As a rule, the requirements cannot be changed after the end of the definition phase. This also applies to designs: the design may not be changed after the design phase has been completed. Should this nonetheless be necessary (which does sometimes occur), the project manager should ensure that the changes are discussed with those involved (particularly the decision-makers or customers) as soon as possible. It is also important that the changes that have been chosen are well documented, in order to prevent later misunderstandings.

Follow-up Phase

Although it is extremely important, the follow-up phase is often neglected. During this phase, everything is arranged that is necessary to bring the project to a successful completion. Examples of activities in the follow-up phase include writing handbooks, providing instruction and training for users, setting up a help desk, maintaining the result, evaluating the project itself, writing the project report, holding a party to celebrate the result that has been achieved, transferring to the directors and dismantling the project team.

The central question in the follow-up phase concerns when and where the project ends. Project leaders often joke among themselves that the first ninety per cent of a project proceeds quickly and that the final ten per cent can take years. The boundaries of the project should be considered in the beginning of a project, so that the project can be closed in the follow-up phase, once it has reached these boundaries.

It is sometimes unclear for those concerned whether the project result is to be a prototype or a working product. This is particularly common in innovative projects in which the outcome is not certain. Customers may expect to receive a product, while the project team assumes that it is building a prototype. Such situations are particularly likely to manifest themselves in the follow-up phase. Consider the case of a software project to test a very new concept.

There was some anxiety concerning whether any results would be produced at all. The project eventually produced good results. The team delivered a piece of software that worked well, at least within the testing context. The customer, who did not know much about IT, thought that he had received a working product. After all, it had worked on his office computer. The software did indeed work, but when it was installed on the computers of fifty employees, the prototype began to have problems, and it was sometimes instable.

Although the programmers would have been able to repair the software, they had no time, as they were already involved in the next project. Furthermore, they had no interest in patching up something that they considered a trial piece. Several months later, when Microsoft released its Service Pack 2 for Windows, the software completely stopped functioning. The customer was angry that the 'product' once again did not work. Because the customer was important, the project manager tried to persuade the programmers to make a few repairs. The programmers were resistant, however, as repairing the bugs would cause too much disruption in their new project. Furthermore, they perceived the software as a prototype. Making it suitable for large-scale use would require changing the entire architectural structure. They wondered if the stream of complaints from the customer would ever stop.

HOW TO MANAGE A PROJECT?

Adopting the six phases creates clarity in a project,

thereby making it easier to administer. What exactly does managing a project entail?

First, project managers and project teams are involved with the following components:

1. *Team.* A project team is comprised of a group of people who will realise the project result. The group is often comprised of people who have various backgrounds, each of whom contributes knowledge and skills.
2. *Goal.* A product result (or goal) is desired. After a project has been completed, something has been realised. A new piece of software has been written, a re-organization has been carried out or a bridge has been built. The project goal is sometimes vague or less firmly established. In many projects, it is necessary to adapt the goal as the project proceeds.
3. *Limited resources.* The amount of time and money that is available for completing a project is always limited. No project is completely free of time pressure.
4. *Uncertainty (risk).* One characteristic feature of projects is that their success is never guaranteed beforehand. Even if the desired goal is already being reached, it is uncertain whether it will be achieved within the available budget or within the proposed time. It is not unusual for a project to take three times as long and to cost twice as much as originally estimated. It is also not unusual for only thirty per cent of the original project team members to be working on the project upon its completion.

Although project managers must attend to many matters, they actually direct projects along only five parameters:

– Time

- Money
- Quality
- Organization
- Information

These five parameters, which are often known as the 'control factors', are described further below. The control factors appear in project plans, progress monitoring and project reporting.

Time

The time factor manifests itself in a project in the form of deadlines for tasks and the amount of time that these tasks may take. Managing time involves ensuring that tasks are completed on time.

Time in project plans:

- Determine which activities should take place in which phase.
- Estimate how long each activity will take
- Determine the order in which activities should be completed.
- Allocate people and materials.
- Allocate activities over time.
- Determine the (most important) deadlines.

Time in progress monitoring:

- Monitor progress.
- Monitor deadlines.
- Adjust schedules.

Time in project reporting:

- Report on the actual timeline.
- Analyse and explain why some tasks proceeded much more quickly or much more slowly than expected.

Time schedules are based on a work-breakdown structure (WBS). A WBS is a decomposition of the tasks that must be completed in order to achieve the project result. Developing a time schedule requires knowing the amount of time that is needed for each task, who will complete each task and when.

When a new project was started, an estimate was made of the number of hours that was thought necessary, but no one ever checked during or after the project to determine whether this number of hours was actually needed. Project managers were nonetheless urged to keep their projects under control. The project leaders protested that, without time records, they had no oversight over the projects. After all, because they had no insight into the number of hours that were used to carry out the tasks of a project, and there was absolutely no chance of adjustment.

One project manager decided to register hours with his team. The registration showed that the project ultimately needed four times as many hours as had been originally estimated. After reprimanding the project manager for allowing the project to get so far out of hand, the management decided to introduce a time-registration system.

After several months, a number of bottlenecks became apparent. It was revealed that nearly all of the projects had been budgeted too narrowly. In practice, personnel who had been assigned to work on a project for one hundred hours often proved to need three times as many hours. This transparency was accompanied by new dilemmas. One the one hand, there were indeed too few personnel to carry out the projects well. Additional personnel were needed. The costs of sufficient personnel were considerable. On the other hand, the projects had apparently been sold far too cheaply (for too few hours) to customers. The management was afraid that they would not receive any more orders if they began to charge more hours in their estimates.

Money

The money factor manifests itself in the project budget. The management of money within a project involves ensuring that the costs remain within the budget. Given that the majority of the costs in most projects are comprised of labour costs, the factors of money and time (the number of labour hours) are closely intertwined.

Money in project plans:

- Determine the fees of the team members.
- Estimate the hours for the team members.
- Assign budgets to team members for specific tasks.
- Determine costs for material and tools.

Money in progress monitoring:

- Monitor cash flow.
- Negotiate with suppliers.
- Determine whether the original cost estimates are still accurate.
- Adjust budgets.
- Negotiate with customer and/or client concerning budget adjustments.

Money in project reporting:

- Compile financial reports and statements.
- Analyse definitive financial report.

Quality

The project result must fulfil a number of quality requirements. This also applies to the various intermediate products of the project. When managing a project, it is particularly important for quality requirements to be determined, agreed upon and recorded in writing during the definition phase. These requirements should never remain implicit. A clear list of requirements can be checked at the end of the implementation phase. This can allow the project team to prove that they have carried out the project according to specifications. Additional quality requirements may be specified for various tasks within the project. For example, a particular task can be carried out only by certified personnel.

Quality in project plans:

- Establish the desired quality of the project result and the intermediate products (this takes place primarily in the definition phase).
- Establish the desired quality of the carrying out of the various activities in the project.

Quality in progress monitoring:

- Test the (intermediate) results.
- Address any quality problems.
- Quality in the project reporting:
- Confirm that the desired quality has been attained.
- Address any complaints (particularly in the follow-up phase).

Perfectionism impedes project management. A pragmatic attitude toward the quality levels of a project can be expressed as 'Good enough is good'. Projects that strive to achieve the highest possible level of quality are often at great risk of never being completed.

Organization

Within a project, the team must be managed. In the

narrowest sense, team management involves determining who will do what from the list of activities.

In broader terms, it also involves all of the soft skills (e.g. motivational techniques, communication skills, leadership styles) that are needed to achieve a goal with a group of people.

Organization in project plans:

- Assemble the team.
- Assign authority.
- Assign tasks to team members.
- Make agreements concerning the availability of people with other (project) managers and higher management.

Organization in progress monitoring:

- Direct the team.
- Monitor human aspects (soft skills).
- Mediate between the parties who are involved in the project.

Information

The information factor concerns how, by whom and on which basis decisions can be taken. Who may decide about which matters in the project? Is it the project leader, the client or a substantive expert within the team? What will be archived and by whom? Will tools (e.g. project website, issue tracker, e-mail notification, joint agenda) be used?

These and other informational questions must be answered before a project can be started. Organizations that regularly work with projects have a number of tools (e.g. Word templates) on hand for handling information within a project.

Information in project plans:

- Which information must be provided to whom and in which form?
- Which information will be recorded, distributed and archived?
- Which information tools will be used?

Information in progress monitoring:

- Arrange for periodic consultation.
- Ensure that the right information is provided to the right person.
- Determine whether agreements have been met.

Information in project reporting:

- Write the project report.

One important aspect of securing the information concerning a project is that all decisions should be reproducible. Decisions are often taken orally and not archived. Regardless of how clear such decisions may seem at the time for both parties, they must eventually appear in writing. If this is not possible, the undocumented decision can become a source of misunderstanding or even conflict. Many projects are delayed by various interventions from outside. Keeping a personal log for recording this type of intervention can help project workers identify the cause of project delays.

Steering the Project in a Meaningful Way

Crucial decisions must be taken at five points during a project; these decision points correspond to the end of each project phase, and they call for recording the project's current status and writing an intermediate report. They also provide the opportunity to reconsider the project phases that are yet to come. At these decision points, project leaders should consult with their clients regarding decisions about the project and adjust the control factors, if necessary. For example, if many new and unexpected requirements have emerged during the definition phase that could increase the costs considerably, it is useless to proceed with the original budget. The decision points at the end of the phases are often 'go/no-go moments'; they call for decisions regarding whether to proceed with the project or whether it should be discontinued.

The following situation often occurs in organisations that do not work according to project phases: a project plan is initially written, in which the control factors are described. A timeline (Time) is specified, and a budget (Money) is prepared, a team is formed (Organization), a goal is described (Quality) and the tools for information services surrounding the project are determined (Information). During a project, the project manager continues to make sure that the project remains somewhat within the total budget and the timeline, but makes no real adjustments. Near the end of a project, the project proves to cost more or to take longer than originally expected. The project is then scaled back to avoid further cost over-runs or delays. Unfortunately, the project result suffers.

Had the project manager in such a case worked with the six-phase model, the team would probably have already concluded in the design phase or perhaps even in the definition phase that the original timeline and budget were insufficient. If the project manager had made adjustments at that time, a simpler design could have been chosen that would have been less expensive and time-consuming to implement. Alternatively, more time, money or both could have been requested from the client. At any rate, the status of the project would have been clear months earlier, and it would have been possible to steer the project in a meaningful way.

2

TOOLS AND TECHNIQUES FOR PROJECT MANAGERS

Project management is a well-established approach to managing and controlling the introduction of new initiatives or organizational changes.

Projects are finite in length, usually one-time pieces of work involving a number of activities that must be completed within a given time frame, and often on a fixed budget. Common examples of projects are construction of a building, introduction of a new product, installation of a new piece of machinery in a manufacturing plant, creation of a new software tool, or the design and launch of a new advertizing campaign.

While the very simplest projects can be managed easily by applying common sense and just getting on with things, projects that are more complex need a great deal of planning, and benefit from a formal, disciplined management approach. From making sure that activities will actually meet the specified need, to devising a workable schedule, developing systems for reporting progress, and managing requests for changes—all of these issues require thoughtful consideration.

Managing projects well requires a great deal of time, skill, and finesse. There are many sides to project management and this is what makes it so interesting and demanding. Project managers are expected to take an uncertain event and make a certain promise to deliver. They are also expected to do this within a specified time and within a limited budget.

TOOLS AND TECHNIQUES

Good managers have a good understanding of best practices for their particular field. This is in the form of methods and techniques that translate knowledge into decisions, insights and actions. They understand what the best companies do and have an ability to interpret what is relevant for their own businesses. The processes they use are generally simple to explain and form a logical step-by-step approach to solving a problem or capturing data and insights. They also encourage creativity—Good managers do not follow a process slavishly where they know they are filling in the boxes rather than looking for insights on how to improve performance. This combination of method and creativity produces the optimum solutions.

They also have a clear understanding of what is important to know and what is simply noise. They either know this information or have it at their fingertips as and when they require it. They also have effective filtering mechanisms so that they don't get overloaded with extraneous information. The level of detail required varies dramatically from one situation to another—the small entrepreneur will work a lot more on the knowledge they have and in gaining facts from quick converzations with experts, whereas a large corporate may employ teams of analysts and research companies. Frequently when a team is going through any process they uncover the need for further data.

Technologies

However, having the facts and understanding best practice will achieve little unless they are built into the systems that people use on a day-today basis. Good managers are good at assessing the relevance of new information technologies and adopting the appropriate ones in order to maximize both effectiveness and efficiency.

Implementation

Finally, having designed the framework that is appropriate to them and their team, Good managers have strong influencing skills and are also great at leading the implementation effort, putting in place the changes necessary to build and sustain the performance of the team.

How tightly or loosely you will use the various tools and techniques will vary, and will to a certain extent depend on personal style. First seek to understand how each could impact you and your team, and then decide what level of change may be appropriate given your starting point, authority and career aspirations.

Each function can take a lifetime to master, but the Good manager will know which areas to focus on—get those areas right and the chances of success improve. Often success relates to the introduction of simple tools and techniques to improve effectiveness and efficiency.

TOP TEN TOOLS AND TECHNIQUES

There are literally thousands of tools and techniques available to the project manager in all areas of project management. Some tools and techniques are so esoteric and specialised that only a few project managers might ever use them, and even then only rarely. Other techniques might only be relevant to certain types of projects. So, which ones to pick?

As you gain experience in project management there will be certain techniques and approaches that will become your 'favourites' and will define your 'style' and approach to management. The integrated project management framework can be seen as your 'project strategy' or process, designed to help in all projects that you manage (figure 1).

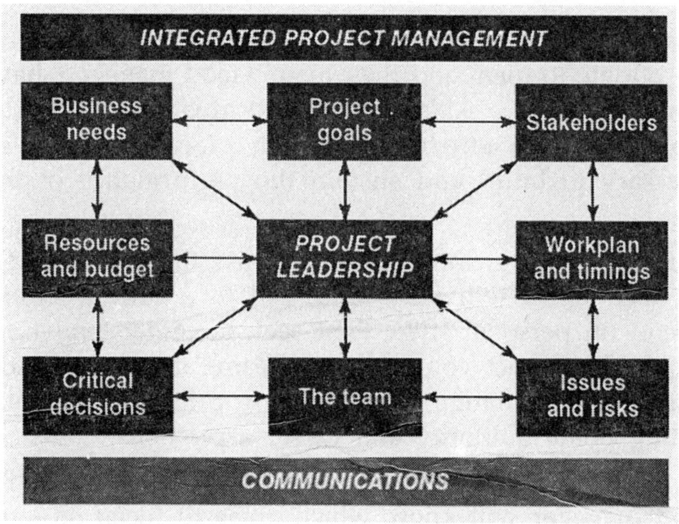

Figure 1. The integrated project management framework

1. Always remembering that projects are a means of delivering value to an organization, it is worth starting with the business needs section and looking at how to create *a project SPRINT* (This acronym stands for situation, problem (or opportunity), risks, impact, needs and timing.*)*.

2. Project goals are closely aligned to business needs, and therefore how to set clear *objectives* is a good skill to possess.
3. Next will look at stakeholders and *stakeholder analysis* as a technique, emphasizing the importance of keeping all key players 'on side'.
4. In the section on workplan and timings there are many techniques to choose from, but have decided to concentrate on *critical path* analysis and calculation as a central tool.
5. In issues and risks a simple technique for *planning contingencies* has always proved useful and can be used for each and every project.
6. In the team look at *selecting* the best people for the job and defining their roles and function.
7. Linked in with this team working, look at how to make critical decisions within projects.
8. Again, there are many tools and techniques for managing resources and budget but a simple way of creating a *project budget* and planning resources is always useful.
9. In terms of project leadership, knowing when and when not to *delegate* is often a key success factor and something that those new to project management may struggle with.
10. Finally, understanding what project communications are all about and how to establish a *communication plan* are always useful, whatever the project.

BUSINESS NEEDS

It must always be remembered that projects are there to deliver value to the organization. In lengthy and complex projects the people involved sometimes simply lose sight of why they are doing what they are doing. Seeing the bigger picture allows those involved in managing and delivering projects to be as flexible as possible at all times, without, however losing the focus on the needs of the business.

For example, once worked with a very large chemicals company which was in the midst of spinning off its 'speciality chemicals' division to a banking-led consortium. There was, therefore, pressure to generate value in that division to get the best price it could. As such, the company was focused on getting as many projects (new products) to completion as possible within a fairly short timescale. The project managers and the ProjectManagement Office (PMO) were consummate professionals who did things according to their book. They were obsessed with 'doing things right' in their own inimical style.

However, a third of the way through a major project, producing a new chemical, competitors launched a similar product. However, because the focus was on 'doing things right', the project continued and the product (well made and excellently project-managed) was brought to market on time, within budget and to the required specification.

The competitors had, however, stolen a march on the chemicals company and its product failed to sell. It was clear that the focus should have been on the business need and 'doing the right thing' (i.e. changing or killing the project) rather than on the detail of managing a project excellently-'doing things right'.

In many organizations people involved are not always even informed as to what the project is about, from a business perspective. They are told what to do and when to do it and possibly even the quality standard pertaining to their task in hand, but they are not given the big picture. If you, as a manager, believe that people will give of their best when asked to achieve something and that your role is to motivate and inspire them, communicating the bigger picture and getting people to understand the business need is crucial.

One of the best ways of ensuring that all projects deliver the value required by a business is to use a checklist so that you do not miss out anything when defining the scope of the project. This checklist ensures that:

- you avoid duplication and gaps in the overall project or programme;
- your project addresses the real need and not what people think has got to happen;
- team members have a common understanding of how the project will deliver value.

One of the most useful checklists at this level is SPRINT. (situation, problem (or opportunity), risks, impact, needs and timing).

Taking every opportunity to build team spirit and commitment, it may be worth getting your core project team together to help go through the SPRINT checklist and then double-checking this with the project sponsor. The core project team in most cases consists of, as a minimum, you, the project manager, your deputy, any sub-project managers and specialists involved for the duration of the project and a representative of the project sponsor or key stakeholder. The SPRINT checklist should help them understand what the project is about. It may be the case that some of these business questions or answers have been created in a brief from the project sponsor or senior management team. In this case, ensure that all key project staff understand what is in that brief and take the time to go back to the source and ask any clarifying questions. Time spent at this early stage in clarifying the business needs is time well spent.

- *Situation.* This is the business situation that necessitates your project. Frame the working of the situation in such a way that all involved in the project can understand it in the context of the project and the organization's goals. In Germany it could be a simple statement such as, 'With high PC ownership there is an opportunity to open up online shopping.' It could also be the results of a business review recommending specific actions such as, 'Open an online retail presence in German as part of expansion into Europe.' In any case, the situation needs to be as clear and unambiguous as possible. The stimulus for the situation statement can come from many sources, such as a political decision or a review of the economic situation, but it needs to be brief, to the point and clear to all.
- *Problem (or opportunity).* What is the problem that the business is facing, or what opportunities are there that the project aims to exploit? These questions allow people to be more flexible and add value to the project as it progresses. The problem could be a statement such as, 'We are not exploiting website for selling purposes,' or restated as an opportunity: 'Develop the website in order to maximize European online sales opportunities.' Obviously, the problem or the opportunity relates to the situation statement.
- *Risks.* These are the risks of *not* doing the project. Don't confuse these risks with the project risks, which will deal with later. Do not over-hype the risks, or the credibility of the project is put at stake, but do demonstrate that if the organization does not do something about the problem or opportunity there will possibly be adverse

ramifications. This could be as simple as stating, 'European sales teams will become demotivated and lose potential bonuses if do not provide online shopping tools for their customers.'

- *Impact.* What will be the quantified impact on the bottom line performance of the business? This is a quantitative assessment of the problem and risks. Some people need figures to help them understand issues, while other people may be more influenced by emotive arguments instead.
- *Needs.* Based on an assessment of the issues the business faces, what is the need or requirement? What is the purpose of the project? The answers to these two questions must link directly to the project's objectives.
- *Timing.* What are the deadlines for satisfying the needs? These should link into the *project statement* and later on into the objectives. A project statement is a single sentence that states what the project is to deliver, by when and within what budget or costs.

It may be impossible to gather all the SPRINT information in one go—for example, at a meeting with all sponsors and the project team. In reality you will probably acquire it over a period of time in smaller meetings before the project starts in earnest. If this is not feasible, you can always allocate what is missing in the project statement to other senior project members and then complete it later.

SETTING CLEAR OBJECTIVES

Essential ingredients for success in project management include defined and agreed goals, a committed team and a viable and flexible plan of action. To achieve your goals, ensure that these essentials are in place. Once you have communicated a vision to the sponsor and team, perhaps using SPRINT, it is time to set clear objectives. Objectives are there to measure the progress and ultimately the success of the project and to support any Go/No Go decisions.

Not all projects have a 'vision statement', but if your project does, you should use this as the basis for explaining what your project is going to do. There is always a degree of interpretation in a vision statement and therefore project objectives should always be checked with the project sponsor and key stakeholders to get consensus on them before you start the implementation. The vision should reflect, for example, the relative importance of time, cost and performance within your project. For instance, 'time to market' might be the prime driver even at the expense of product functionality or cost.

How do you ensure that project objectives are clear and valid?

– List the objectives you wish to achieve or have elicited from the vision statement.

– Try to avoid listing an activity instead of an objective. For example, 'Complete a pilot' does not really answer the question 'Why?' Instead 'Complete a pilot to demonstrate that the project will achieve its planned business impact with minimal risk of spoiling the market' is an objective rather than an action.

– Try to make the objectives measurable. If you are having difficulty with this, then ask yourself: 'How will know that have achieved this objective?'

– The objectives will probably be debated by a number of people. Therefore use them as a 'straw man' to discuss with key stakeholders what the project is about and what the objectives should be.

Making Objectives

SMART is an acronym that has become very popular with individuals wishing to set clear objectives. However, while many people know what the acronym stands for (or variants thereof), few actually understand what that actually means to the objectives in question. Here, define the SMART acronym as:

— *Specific.* So what does specific mean when it comes to setting objectives? For many it means separating multiple objectives out into individual ones and making them detailed and clear. Linking objectves to the business need also ensures that they are specific.

— *Measurable.* Putting a figure on something makes it easier to measure, but this in itself causes some issues for the project manager. Generally, most objectives are either quantitative or qualitative by nature. Objectives that measure time, cost and outputs tend to be quantitative and therefore not subjective. There is usually a common understanding of these types of objective and the way in which they are measured (the metrics). However, a problem arises when qualitative, subjective elements are included in objectives. Then there needs to be a common understanding of the qualities these objectives are trying to measure and how to measure them. The study of quality management has generated many ways of 'measuring' quality, but for the new project manager the rule seems to be—get a common understanding beforehand of what is meant by 'quality'. If the project requires an objective to be about something that is difficult to put a figure on—for example, happiness, user-friendliness or motivation—ask stakeholders why these qualities are important and how they would know at the end of the project whether they have been achieved.

Some managers categorically insist that if an objective cannot be measured then it has no place as a project objective—it is not 'objective'. Others point to the fact that not all projects are as cut and dried as that and some subjectivity has to be part of the project to add value. The trap that both proponents can fall into is that they end up spending more time setting up a means to measure the objectives and performance than is wise—and ironically end up reducing the actual value of the project.

- *Agreed.* A fundamental prerequisite for focusing a team and getting it to pull together is a common, agreed, objective. Therefore, in most variants of the SMART acronym 'agreed' has a key part to play. This requires the objectives to be understood by all the stakeholders after a degree of discussion and debate. Ultimately, all concerned must agree to the objectives in order to get the full commitment of people and resources within the team and other stakeholders outside.
- *Realistic.* For a project to be achievable, the objectives must be realistic. But how do you know whether something is realistic or not? For most project managers, something is realistic when the following are taken into account. Only when you have assessed all the factors below and found them to be positive can the objective be said to be 'realistic':
  1. Time—is there enough time to get the project done?
  2. Resources—is there a budget and resources (including having the necessary skills and knowledge) to do the job?

3. Other commitments—what else are project managers and key resources committed to?

– *Time bound.* To drive performance, all objectives should have a deadline associated with them. These should be linked to the other SMART elements and also linked to the project statement. For example, in UK a cutting edge manufacturer of domestic appliances, with over 10 per cent of its workforce dedicated to development projects based on its patented approach to cleaning, managed to bring only one new product to market in seven years. It managed to produce over 28 variants of its existing technology and products, but it was always seen as a 'one-trick pony'. On analyzing why this was the case, it was found that the founder and CEO was unable to stop tinkering with the technical objectives of projects underway and therefore 'scope creep' became almost endemic. A bad project should be stopped as soon as possible, but it is almost an equal crime to keep moving the goalposts of a good project in a constant attempt to make things better.

There are many other ways of setting, categorizing and detailing project objectives and many debates about, for example, the number of objectives any project should have. However, for the Good project manager the SMART tool can put the project on a good footing. Time spent on getting project objectives right is time well spent and will benefit the project manager towards the end of the project.

STAKEHOLDER ANALYSIS

Talking through many a project 'war story' with project managers, are always surprised when the matter of 'office politics' raises its head with a project being 'killed off due to someone 'not liking it' or it 'clashing with their interests'. After many years of hearing this wondered whether there is anything a project manager could do to offset the risk of a project clashing with the 'vested interest' within a business. Stakeholder analysis was the answer.

Stakeholder analysis is a name that can be ascribed to a series of techniques whose aim is to understand the key players involved in the business environment and their attitude towards your project. Traditionally had always thought of stakeholders as being generally either positive or benign towards projects. However, working with the NHS showed Simon how not all stakeholders can be seen as positive and, as such, steps need to be taken well in advance to understand these 'negative' stakeholders and do something accordingly.

Use stakeholder analysis carefully. Because are dealing here with individual attitudes and feelings, stakeholder analysis must be dealt with very carefully and thought through in advance. Some people prefer to remove names from the matrix and put in letters instead to make the technique anonymous.

Carry out the stakeholder analysis at the very start of the project, while formulating and discussing objectives. It should link to the communication plan and consider how stakeholders are kept informed of project progress. There is no guarantee that by using the tool your project will never fall foul of office intrigue and manipulation, but at least by using it you improve your project communication and personalise it. Basically you are trying to pre-empt opposition, assess the risks such opposition brings and reduce those risks.

A US East Coast bank was working on a new internet banking product. The project team had been in place for three months and a reasonable amount of funds had been invested in the project to date. During a project conference call, facilitated by Patrick, one of the participants stated that the project would have to be 'canned'. If the project manager and team had looked into who had the influence and power over all things internet-related they would have saved themselves months of work or at least got one of the key players on board at the very beginning in order to save the project. It was never fully understood whether his objectives were truly technical or personal, but in any case the project stayed canned.

WORKPLAN AND TIMINGS

One of the few tools and techniques that is essential to a project manager looking to shorten or 'crunch' the project plan is critical path analysis. However, although it is often mentioned, it is not always completely understood. Many managers understand how to create the critical path within a project but do not fully realise the benefits of this technique and what it can do for them.

In the planning phase of a project, not all activities can, or need, to start at the same time to meet the project's planned completion date. Some activities will be critical to completing the project on time; if they slip by a week then the whole project will slip by a week. Project planners and managers use critical path analysis to identify these activities.

Critical Path

The critical path is the path through the network of tasks that shows the minimum time needed to finish the project. Software makes life a lot easier for calculations, but understanding the basics to calculate the critical path can really help a project manager and key stakeholders. A few basic techniques will enable you to calculate manually and understand the critical path and its value to you and the project.

1. Complete a list of all the activities required to complete the project. Look at how they interrelate.
2. Decide which activities have to start immediately or first, which next, and then work through all the tasks until the end of the list
3. Because some activities can happen in parallel, create a network diagram. This diagram shows the relationship between activities and their dependencies. The diagram can be simple or complex, according to how many activities there are and the number of 'paths' through the project. If you are new to network diagrams, do not underestimate the power of the Post—it note in planning. Write an activity on each Post-it note, and then, using a flat surface, lay all the Post—ts out in a logical sequence or order remembering that some tasks can be done in parallel.
4. Indicate durations of each task and add up the total time required to complete each route ('path') through the network. The longest route is known as the critical path, which shows the shortest possible duration for the project.

Once you know the critical path you can understand many other elements of planning your project and the resources required. You can:

— calculate the start and end dates of the project (add the start date to the critical path total duration and you have a finish date; or, if you prefer, take the project deadline and subtract the total duration of the critical path to create the start date—usually this is the point at which you find out you should have started a week ago);

– use the network diagram to find opportunities for shortening the project schedule by looking at where you can cut task times on activities on the critical path;
– use resources wisely by understanding that tasks not on the critical path have some 'slack time' and that allocating resources to these tasks to reduce the overall project duration will not work;
– understand the progress of the project by closely monitoring the tasks on the critical path, since delays in these tasks will delay the whole project;
– schedule non-critical path tasks and delay or advance them according to progress;
– tailor your project diary to ensure that you are supervizing the tasks on the critical path as a priority, as opposed to spending time on tasks of less importance.

We are constantly amazed as to why intelligent senior managers seem to think that throwing resources at a project will result in a quicker result. Time after time resources, blood, sweat and tears are spent on tasks that are not on the critical path. Yet management still believe that speeding up those individual tasks will benefit the whole project. A simple explanation of the critical path and how it works and an understanding of the concept of slack time are often all that is needed for senior managers to take a more considered view of allocating resources to speed up projects.

PLANNING CONTINGENCIES

Well-constructed plans all have at least one thing in common—they all come up against unexpected and changing circumstances. Just because you have activities scheduled in, it doesn't mean they will go according to plan. As a result, good project managers should apply some basic risk management principles to their project and plans.

However, it is not possible to pre-empt every eventuality that could harm the project. It is, therefore, good practice to get the core project team to consider what it will do if certain threats become reality so as to minimize the impact of them. This is, in essence, contingency planning. There are many very complex risk management tools and techniques that can be employed by the project manager today. However, just understanding the basics can really help.

Contingency action plans are there to address the effects of a risk once it has become reality. They are not there to minimize the chance or probability of something happening, but to reduce the effects. You may never use them, but there is a risk you may have to, so plan them in advance. It's as simple as making a decision about an umbrella. You need to take an umbrella with you when going for a walk in case it rains. It's no use when getting wet wishing you had picked up your umbrella on the way out. On the other hand, you may never need the umbrella, so having it may seem an unnecessary burden or expense.

Contingency Plan

Contingency plans should be part of a full risk management approach, including assessments of risks and pre-emptive actions. However, as a basic, quick tool, try the following process:

1. Discuss the threats to the project plan regularly with the core team and prioritise and decide which threats need the most attention.
2. Be specific and focus upon the top few risks and think through, perhaps with subject matter experts, the possible effects of a risk if it occurs.

3. Create a formal contingency plan and cost it up with whoever supplies the necessary resources.
4. Set a formal 'trigger' with those in charge of the contingency plan. The trigger is an action, event or date whereby the contingency plan is put into action. All involved should know what this trigger is, as without it the contingency plan is useless and has become a waste of resources.
5. Document the contingency plan and triggers and keep them with the project documentation. This information will feed into the next project you do and help in planning future risk management strategies. The plan and triggers should be part of your risk register.

Remember that the more stakeholders involved in planning for contingencies, the better the plan. If there is a very strong likelihood that the contingency plan will need to be put into action, then factor it into the project plan in advance so that it becomes part of the plan. Time spent on validating the plan and preparing for problems in advance is rarely time wasted. As a project manager, you should double-check the entire contingency plan before you start to implement the project.

If this, admittedly rather pessimistic, mindset was employed by all project managers, would there be a lot less surprises in projects?

TEAM SELECTION

Remember, it is people that make projects successful, not software or systems. So any project manager will want to select the best people for the job and use them effectively. However, many managers feel that they have little leeway when it comes to selecting members of their core project team—they have whom they have and there is very little choice. In addition, many project managers find that they don't have enough people to fill distinctive specialist project roles and that a number of people will have to double up in their roles.

Despite these limitations, it is worth having a look at the techniques that could support you as a project manager in the area of team selection. Build your team carefully, since it will make or break the project. When you have found the person with the right skills, ask yourself:

- How this person well enough to trust them?
- Is it possible to work comfortably with them?
- Will they get along with the other team members?
- Do they have the skills needed or will they require some training?

Think about a very successful project that you have been part of in the past (come on, there must be one!). Then think about the project manager of that successful project and list the skills and abilities of that manager and how they directly contributed to the success of the project. Once you have written them down, divide the skills and abilities into two types—those of a technical nature (e.g. planning skills, content knowledge of the project, risk management skills) and those of an interpersonal nature (e.g. good motivator, good communication skills, empathy, excellent delegation skills). You should find that the effective project manager has a combination of both types of skill -technical and interpersonal.

It is a well-known fact that people tend to recruit in their own image. People may have the necessary technical skills for the job but if everyone is technical by nature or training there is a risk that the team may not have much in the way of people skills, or *vice versa*.

Assess your core team's abilities—are they all technical geniuses but not that comfortable standing up and talking to people and listening to their ideas, or are they the opposite—great empathisers but with little or no content knowledge of the project on hand and no planning skills whatsoever? If this is the case then you need to move towards a balance. Start recruiting to your team people whose skills and, more importantly, abilities complement yours, rather than duplicate them.

Team Roles

In any team you need to look for people to carry out a team role as well as their functional role. To operate efficiently you, as the team leader and project manager, will want someone to perform the following roles:

- *Coordinator/administrator.* Someone who pulls together the work of the team as a whole and keeps all the paperwork/IT databases up to date.
- *Critic.* The guardian and analyst of the team's effectiveness, who challenges people when standards and quality drop.
- *Ideas person.* Someone who innovates and looks for new ways of doing things and for potential shortcuts.
- *Implementer.* A person who ensures that the team's actions and decisions are put into place and are seen through.
- *External contact.* Someone who oversees external contacts and relations with third parties.
- *Inspector.* The quality guru who looks to ensure that a project has high quality throughout and that the team works to high standards. The inspector should always seek to establish new standards and ways of working which raise standards. In contrast

to the critic, the inspector should always cite alternatives and options.

- Expert. The technical specialist required for certain parts of the project or for detailed analysis. There may be more than one.

As you appoint people to the team, check off each of these roles to make sure that someone in the team leans towards that sort of contribution. You may discuss this team role with them or not, depending on circumstances (and politics).

Build a team that takes advantage of each individual's skills and avoids the impact of their weaknesses. Remember, especially if you are involved with projects for third parties or external clients, you should ask potential team members if they identify with the aims and objectives of the project. They do not have to agree with them totally but they must at least feel comfortable with why the organization needs to achieve them.

We are increasingly aware that seniority and job description do not always determine competence, and that when forming a team attitude and dependability count for a lot. In a London-based banking corporation a series of tasks within a major project required the gathering of information from a number of directors and senior managers. She took it as an insult on her professional integrity if tasks she asked for were late—irrespective of who the person involved was. Many of the directors and managers involved knew of her and were anxious not to cross her. In terms of getting things done, she was excellent. She was not the most senior member of the team by any means, and she did not have the technical skills for the specific tasks. Yet she had tenacity, and people were concerned about not getting her work done on time. She was the best team member for that part of the project.

MAKING DECISIONS AS A TEAM

Whether in the planning or implementation phase of your project, quality decision-making is crucial. New project managers may wish to involve members of the team in making important decisions but this can be fraught with difficulties. Using a decision-making process gets over such problems. Using a formal process may seem over the top at first, and look as though it takes up too much time, but speed will improve with experience. Most importantly, a quality consultative process will help you come to the right decision. The spin-off benefit is that people implement decisions more willingly if they feel that they have been part of the decision-making process.

So, having a logical process is the key to good, team decisions. The only potential drawback, apart from the time issue, is that there is sometimes a risk of 'group-think', where everyone involved comes up with a similar answer or recommendation just when you wanted people to think differently and more widely.

Decision-making Process

Here is a simple process for team decision-making.

1. The team must first agree on the criteria against which to measure a decision or course of action. Ask team members to brainstorm what an ideal solution would look like, using questions such as, What benefits should look for in a solution?' or What should any solution do for us?' This list of criteria can then give you and the team a way of filtering options and comparing the alternatives.
2. The next stage is to identify which criteria are the most important. You are looking for the vital criteria against which any alternative option will be judged—the minimum standard.

3. Now measure all the options available against the ideal agreed for each criterion. This seems easy but actually requires creativity to evaluate possible decisions effectively.
4. Continue this measurement and evaluations process until one option stands out. Encourage debate and discussion at this stage, as you need input from all involved.
5. Look at this 'final' option—what are the risks around this alternative and how do they weigh against the potential benefits? If the risks are acceptable and the option meets your decision-making objectives, then go for it. It is your best-balanced decision.

As an example, in the planning phase of a project teams often have to decide which suppliers or contractors to use. Setting clear criteria for how to make those choices will give the team a good start. Understanding which criteria are the most important—cost, speed, quality or a combination of other factors—is critical to helping a team come to a swift decision. Then you can measure the performance of possible suppliers against these criteria to narrow down the available options. Keep discussing the options, refining as you go the criteria and the standards you require against them. This brings you to the best option, and you need quickly to examine the risks that this decision might involve. At the end of the process not only should you have the best decision but also you will have the team's agreement to the decision and their commitment to their role in implementing it.

In many projects, once the decision and choice has been made, the reasons behind it are often lost. In contrast, in a forward-looking learning organization the criteria for decision-making are often kept as a guide for future teams.

You might want an objective critic, who is not part of the core project team, at this stage to review your decision before you implement it— acting as a final 'double-check'. This is important, for as project manager the final responsibility rests with you. Here's a double-checking shortcut that validates the choice using the SAFE acronym:

- *Suitable.* Is the decision really the most suitable one, given the current state of the project?
- *Acceptable.* Is the decision acceptable to all the key stakeholders who have an interest in the project—not just those involved in making the decision?
- *Feasible.* Will the implementation of the decision be practical and feasible, given time, resources and skills available?
- *Enduring.* Will the solution or course of action decided upon endure to the end of the project and into the long term, or is it just a short-term solution?

CREATING A PROJECT BUDGET

When it comes to finances and budgeting, many people—particularly technical project managers—start to worry. It is not their natural ground to cost up a project; but until you create a full project budget there is no way of calculating whether the project will generate a positive return on investment (ROI). It is unlikely that a project will be given authorization to go ahead without an accurate and detailed idea of costs, yet people seem to think that they can fudge financial planning. What you need is a basic tool to work out costs for a project—the resources matrix.

Create a matrix showing all the activities that make up the project, and the resources required, broken down by type, the amount required and the cost. The headings in the matrix should be relevant to your project. Include a 'special' column to record and cost up all resources that are unique or highly costly to your project or may have a long lead time. Costing them up separately is a way of highlighting their value to the project.

There may be a good reason to separate the capital costs (one-off expenditure subject to depreciation) from the revenue costs (materials, services and people costs). In either case, the bottom of the matrices should be combined to get a working estimate of the costs of the project. This figure should be added to the project statement and will give any senior management reviewing the project an idea of whether the project is cost effective. It also gives the accountants the opportunity to calculate the return on investment (ROI).

Without a full breakdown of the costs, human and other, it is impossible for stakeholders to assess what the ROI will be. Many companies break down their capital costs, ignoring their staff costs, and although they deliver the project they never get round to comparing the short-term costs of delivering the project against the long-term benefits of the project. Very little project measurement ever gets done afterwards. When ask companies why this is so, usually get the answer that people are already busy on the next project and have no time to go back over the results and compare them against the planned costs. Generally, these organizations never improve the projects they do—but they still carry on delivering projects, some with real, unmeasured, value and some with none.

If you are not happy with figures, and many managers are not, then always try to check the numbers with a project cost accountant. Use standard costs and figures where available, and check how your company treats overheads as project charges.

PROJECT DELEGATION

What activities should you delegate within your project and what should you never delegate? Remember the golden rule—you can delegate *authority* to someone else for a part of the project but ultimately the *responsibility* for the delivery of the project always remains with you, the project manager. It is a poor project manager who hides behind their people when, for example, mistakes are made.

There are many tools for managers to use in delegating work to others but the question of what you should delegate can be tricky. From a business perspective you should delegate anything that can be done quicker, better and cheaper by someone else apart from you. However there are a number of tasks that should not be passed on to others, no matter how competent those people may be. These include:

- *Praise.* It rather dilutes the effect if you ask others to thank people on your behalf. Always make the effort to thank people personally—either by phone, email or face to face. Asking other people to give out your praise sends quite a contrary message—you value their efforts and hard work but not quite enough to thank them personally.
- *Reward.* This is an extension of praise in a more material way. Giving rewards is always the preserve of line managers, and this means that within the context of a project it is the preserve of the project manager.
- *Issues of discipline.* Managing disciplinary matters is not just about managing poor performance or poor quality of work but also about addressing issues that affect the working and results of the project team. As project manager, you should deal with these directly.

- *Managing the sponsor.* Managing the relationship with the sponsor has to be done by the project manager. You cannot delegate this key management relationship.
- *Confidentiality.* If people have requested a degree of confidentiality on an issue or your personal guarantee of secrecy then delegation is clearly not an option—if you wish to retain credibility.

Patrick was once called into an organization to help get a project back on track and was confronted by a very stressed-out project manager. He was clearly an expert in the project subject but it soon became clear that because he was so expert he felt that no one could do the work as well as he and therefore he did not delegate. Other members of staff also recognized his expertise and a vicious circle ensued where other people did not offer their help as they knew that their knowledge was not at the same level as the expert project manager. The project manager rapidly became the project 'doer'. He got involved in every piece of detail and lost the big picture. He did try to delegate work but either found it difficult to explain what he required or complained that it was just as quick to do it himself.

He was quite right. In the very short term delegation does not save time. However, in the medium to long term, making the effort to explain what is required and to what level will save time. The danger is that as the project falls behind schedule the project manager feels they have even less time to delegate work, and so on and so on.

Delegating Effectively

Delegation is all about the distribution of work or management to make things more effective or efficient. It is therefore crucial to delegate tasks in a way that minimizes the chance of confusion or miscommunication. Your project management approach must seek to clarify tasks, outline objectives and improve communication. By doing this, and focusing upon making all tasks clear and measurable, you will make the task of delegation easier. With practice, delegation becomes natural and you may even get a reputation as a project manager that allows your staff the freedom to act independently within the project. This has great benefits when trying to attract the best people in your organization to your projects. They know they are going to be trusted to get on with it and that they are going to learn and develop.

It can be useful to subdivide a project into a number of sub-projects as well as tasks. A sub-project is a discrete piece of work within a project, which when combined with the other tasks completes the whole project. Identifying sub-projects can be a powerful medium for delegation, giving responsibility to another team member for a discrete sub-objective of the project.

As well as making sure that the tasks you have delegated are SMART, a simple checklist will help to ensure that you are on the right track:

1. Check that the task is suitable for delegation in the first place. Make sure it is not one of the tasks that is essential for you to do. In a project environment, most tasks are delegated for reasons of resource efficiency and/or technical ability. You need someone to do something because of your lack of time and/or skills.
2. Make sure that the individuals or teams who you have in mind have the necessary skills, abilities, attitude and time to do what you ask. In a project environment, as opposed to 'business as usual', you will not have time to train or develop others to

make them suitable for some tasks that you would like to delegate. This is a test of the skills sets that have been part of your selection criteria when choosing project team members.

3. Part of the 'contract' in delegating work is an explanation of what is being delegated and why. The 'why' should include an element of 'why them?' and 'what's in it for them?'. Make sure you explain how the tasks fit in with the project objectives.
4. Clearly state the desired results. This means setting quality standards, timescales, deadlines and your definition of success. The clearer this is, the greater the chance of success, first time.
5. As part of defining the desired results, there should be some discussion of the resources available for the task at hand. There may be some leeway for change at this stage, but often resources have already been agreed and there may be very little room for manoeuvre. Make that clear as well, to avoid the person delegated coming to you for more resources as they carry out the task.
6. Give ongoing support. While avoiding the temptation to interfere is crucial, it is necessary for you, the project manager, to ensure that the person or persons you have delegated to know how and when they can access you for any reason. Agreeing a means by which you can monitor progress will also avoid the charge of interfering during the task period. Remember, you are delegating not abdicating.
7. Review performance. Ideally, as soon as the delegated tasks have been completed the project manager should review performance with those people delegated to do the task. However in

reality, this is often left until the end of the project or phase. The key is that it should be done, and as soon as practicable.

Delegation does not have to be limited to physical tasks. The delegation of the management of tasks or parts of the project is where experienced project managers free up more time. This comes with experience, but using tools like the resources matrix and the responsibility assignment matrix will make the delegation of management easier.

Delegation isn't the only skill required of project managers and leaders—they also need to be able to inspire, motivate and take a high-level view. But without delegation, less time will be available to focus on these other skills.

PROJECT COMMUNICATION PLAN

For a project to run smoothly, the resources required must be available at the time you need them. This demands planning—of people, facilities, equipment and resources. Think of the communication plan as being a subset of the project plan.

It is important to make information available to the people who need it, when they need it and in the right format. Your challenge as a project manager is to facilitate and encourage this communication within and outside the project team. Ensure that all project data is up to date and recorded efficiently—this will then allow you to disseminate information as required. The ideal is to have a Project Management Office (PMO) for managing multiple projects, but on a smaller scale a knowledge centre is equally valuable—often known as the 'war room'.

Knowledge Centre

Remember that each item of project information has some potential value to someone. In most cases it will be obvious what needs to be stored, but try to think more widely and take a longer view. Could this seemingly trivial piece of information be of value to another project manager after this project has finished? In this age of high-speed information technology and bandwidth, there is no reason not to store something due to lack of capacity.

Appoint a coordinator to be in charge of managing all the information. They should be responsible for getting the data in from team members and giving out the right data at the right time in the right format to the stakeholders. This data could be, for example, Gantt charts, activity reports, risk registers or issue logs. A good project administrator is usually the sole person in charge of the version control process, and in well-managed projects this administrator will issue the latest, common, up-to-date version of the Gantt chart for all to see.

There is also a risk that the project team gets swamped with data, so think about the following in advance.

1. What data do require to manage the project and how shall classify it? Try classifying information by dividing data into the following categories:
   - *General planning information:* Objectives, vision statement, master schedule, network diagrams.
   - *General data:* Background information that might be useful to carry out activities.
   - *Completed activities:* Data gathered on finished tasks.
   - *Activities in progress:* Data required for people carrying out activities now.

- *Activities not yet started:* Data that might be useful for up and coming tasks and activities.

2. Who needs what data, when and in what format? Apart from the members of the project team, who should have access to the knowledge centre? There are also probably others outside the organization who could benefit from information you can share.
   - Refer to the list of stakeholders you made at the start of the project as part of the stakeholder analysis.
   - Categorise those who are crucial to the project and therefore will get data as a priority.
   - Plan how you are going to make the data available. It could be 'push'—i.e. sending data out to them, which requires your active management at specific times—or 'pull'—i.e. posting data somewhere for them to find. The rule should be that this takes as little time as possible for you or your knowledge coordinator to manage.
   - Review the format of the data, the timings and the content with the stakeholders and team members.

Knowledge and information are the oil that keeps the project running smoothly, but in general people do not appreciate this until they feel 'out of the loop'.

PROJECT MANAGEMENT AND LEADERSHIP

For many years projects were seen as single operations following strict rules of specification, time and budget, but this view is being overtaken by the notion that projects are the means for much more comprehensive change which involves many more unknowns. Many organizations have now grouped projects with their own specific goals into programmes with broadly common objectives. In this way companies have moved up a gear and started to 'manage by projects', in order to deliver higher-order strategic objectives, which would not be possible if the projects were treated independently. Further, as the number of projects and project programmes within companies grows, the emphasis shifts to the management of the total 'portfolio of projects', implying that as strategic imperatives change new projects may be created and earlier ones terminated, regardless of individual project viability against its initial objectives. In consequence project managers now need to pay attention to three dimensions: thinking 'inwards' on how to be successful with their single project; thinking 'upwards' on the strategic fit for their project; and thinking 'sideways' on how their single project may be combined with other projects to form a better project portfolio.

A widening of the scope of projects, and, at the same time, the use of the project concept for a broadening range of activities (including both physical projects and 'soft areas' such as organizational change), has led to a shift in thinking about the role of projects in a modern society. There is an increasing recognition that projects act as 'influencing agents' instead of being a reaction to societal trends. This has led to three particular concerns for organizations:

1. The extent to which the projects' base organization is mature enough to handle a range of highly complex projects, so that it can provide adequate support.
2. The existence of a strong belief in the benefits of using projects for implementing change.
3. The degree to which there is a climate among its stakeholder group for active knowledge-building

relating to the impact of projects.

Project maturity within the business community is the sum of the ability to act and a willingness to be involved, and an understanding of the impact of project willingness and project action. Understanding, knowledge, learning and acting are closely related and will play an active and interactive role in building a desired attitude for change through projects.

The division of labour and the rationality of the decision process, together with good lines of communication and a well understood and accepted authority structure, enhance the operational capability. Projects will be best managed when they have a mix of 'cultural' and 'structural' elements embodied in the project process. The principle that risk has to be treated differently depending on the level within the organization seems, then, to be valid for projects in general.

At lower levels, risks are within the control of the key project actors and should be handled by them, while risks at higher levels can only be handled appropriately through an understanding of projects in relation to both the strategy of the company or the organization and, at the same time, the external environment seen from a wider angle. That projects should be part of a hierarchy within an organization in order to be handled professionally is a very important message today just as at the individual level major operations can only be understood when put into a strategic framework.

A second concern is how, then, to measure real project success. Traditionally project success was viewed narrowly as the achievement of intended outcomes in terms of specification, time and budget. While this was widely accepted in early notions of project management, when the project context shifted it became apparent that a broader set of outcome measures was needed. Such influences include the growing concern to ensure maximization of the lifetime value of the project endeavour, the notion of the sustainable enterprise, the importance of knowledge as the source of competitive advantage, and the importance of motivation as a source for better project execution. Within knowledge-based enterprises, projects are today being considered as important arenas for learning; the uniqueness of each project makes project work rich in personal and organizational learning opportunities.

So, in modern projects, success is a broad concept that deals with the impact of the project overall, i.e. both project management success and project end-product success. Expanding the success criteria in this way will necessarily postpone the final judgement of the project—often months or years after the completion of the project itself—to include lifetime performance measures.

Given this broader set of expected outcomes it is obvious that project management needs to respond rather differently than before. Both policy-makers and project managers can benefit from understanding the interrelationship of factors that need particular attention, in order to achieve these outcomes and the eventual establishment of new performance indicators for the management of projects.

The third area of particular concern has to do with the way projects are executed. There has long been recognition that ICT (Information and Communication Tecchnology) has influenced way of thinking and behaving. Technology has not only relieved us of much boring, repetitive work, enabling us to focus attention on more advanced, innovative and creative thinking, but it has also made us able to do things faster and more comprehensively than ever before.

For projects, this development has had a strong influence on project execution and control, replacing the old notion that operations can be undertaken in a logical series of steps. Decision-making based on a time-consuming and linear process of data collection, analysis, elaboration, then conclusions and then perhaps publication and action has been significantly compressed and rapid decision processes made possible. The 'scrum' concept has emerged for project execution. Borrowed from baseball and later refined using the 'action research and action learning' principle, it recommends stand-up-meetings on an every-morning basis, in sequences of three to four weeks, where project teams are invited to bring in new developments and thoughts, and change the project process where appropriate. Project control is normally closely related to the project plan, hence the measures adopted fail to take into account the extent the project processes are using the latest developments in the field.

❖❖❖

3

TECHNICAL EXPERTISE OF EFFECTIVE PROJECT MANAGERS

Information technology and information systems are powerful and valuable tools for all aspects of management. When applied thoughtfully, these tools can bring important benefits for individuals, organizations, and customers. When misapplied, they can waste tremendous amounts of time, effort, and money. In the world of globalization, Information system is such where data are collected, classified and put into process interpreting the result thereon in order to provide an integrated series of information for further communicating and analyzing. In a progressively more spirited worldwide atmosphere, information technology plays the role as 'enabler and facilitator', which endows with tactical values to the officialdom and considerable step up to the excellence of administration.

It was not that long ago that a printed out Project Charter would be the start of project approval. The key stakeholders would physically sign the document, which would be passed in the internal mail between parties, finally returning to the project manager to update the version control for the document to version 1.0. She would then file it away for safe-keeping and proof that the initiation phase was over and that the real work could begin. Most project sponsors would now expect the entire approvals process to be done by email. That is not to say that you can skip getting formal project approval. Instead, the way you go about securing sponsor sign off is different, due to the technology available to you—and them—in the workplace. No longer do project managers have a filing cabinet of original functional specs and documents signed off in ink. They are more likely to hot desk with limited storage space for project files. Documentation is stored electronically on a central shared server, with scanned copies of any documentation that has been signed. Copies of approval emails are stored with the rest of the project documents on the server. This is now the accepted ways of working, even in industries like financial services which typically take a while to catch up.

This approach to handling documentation has evolved due to the availability of technology of work, and an evolution of the way in which we use it. This has given risen to the 'Google generation'. You probably fall into this category. It is not to do with age. It is a distinction based on the adoption of new technology. If you want information, you can go to Google (or any other search engine), type your question and get a relevant response in a fraction of a second. The search engines has changed the way project stakeholders expect to get information.

In other words, if you need to find something out, you expect to be able to do so quickly and conveniently. It is no longer necessary to trawl through encyclopædias or take a trip to the library to do research. If you don't know the answer, you can search the question on your computer or mobile phone. This phenomena has contributed the rise of cheating in pub quizzes, but it has also made project management more difficult.

In the past—and it wasn't that long ago—the monthly steering group report would be an adequate representation of the project status. It was acknowledged that it was not a real-time project position, but it was accurate enough for the purposes of judging progress against milestones and budget. This data would be sufficient for steering group, and if anyone else wanted a formal project status report, the latest steering group report could be handed over as a snapshot in time. Most of the time, people were happy with this level of detail, even though implicitly they knew it could no longer be true. Only in an emergency would any one ask to see anything more up to date.

Today, project stakeholders have different expectations about project information, because they can get other information at the click of button. You want to know the weather in Bangalore? Search it. You want real-time stock prices on the FTSE? Search it. You want up to date project status reports. Here's last month's steering group report, precisely 19 days out of date. This lack of real-time data is no longer acceptable to project stakeholders who can get everything else in a fraction of a second.

The fact that people are connected at work and at home has a knock-on impact on the way in which we provide project data. Now project stakeholders expect real-time, up to date status reports. Or at least, they expect you to give them that information whenever they ask for it, by return of email. Project managers now have to deal with those raised expectations and always be on top of project status in case anyone asks.

Project managers who don't know what is going on—and are not able to communicate it—aren't serving the needs of the project team or the wider stakeholder community. Of course, accurate and timely information works both ways, and we need it from sponsors too.

To remain as effective and efficient as possible, good managers differentiate themselves by the support mechanisms they put in place to help themselves and their team. These include the intelligent use of appropriate technologies—enabling, for example, the automation of non-core activities, thereby freeing up time to focus on managing, motivating and leading people. They may also include the use of coaches, peer-to-peer networks, and gaining access to the latest thinking in the field. However, information technology, especially in the sphere of project and programme management, can, if badly managed, often get in the way of effective management rather than support it.

ROLE OF TECHNOLOGY IN PROJECT MANAGEMENT

Technology at its best can be an enabler. It can help the project manager cope with the rapid rate of change in the external environment by keeping them abreast of changes in the relevant sector or business. In a complex business and within a multifunctional project, how can a project manager possibly hope to keep up to date and remain aware of what is going on?

There is certainly no shortage of information channels, from social networking sites and blogs to specialist forums and special interest groups—frankly, there is too much. How do project managers sift through the myriad of emails, websites, reports, conference calls and mobile texts that arrive at all times of the day and night?

While information overload is a critical issue, the reality is that if don't make use of relevant and up-to-date information then will fall behind the competition. While technology is not the answer to all problems, it is a very important enabler to help us remain effective and efficient-especially within project management.

Time Saving

Before deciding how to use automation/technology to save time, first you need to eliminate entirely low-value or unnecessary activities.

Make a list of everything you do on a week-to-week basis. Assess how much time is spent on each, as well as the value you associate with each—perhaps using a simple five-point scale. Then draw a simple two by two matrix to assess where each activity falls in Figure below.

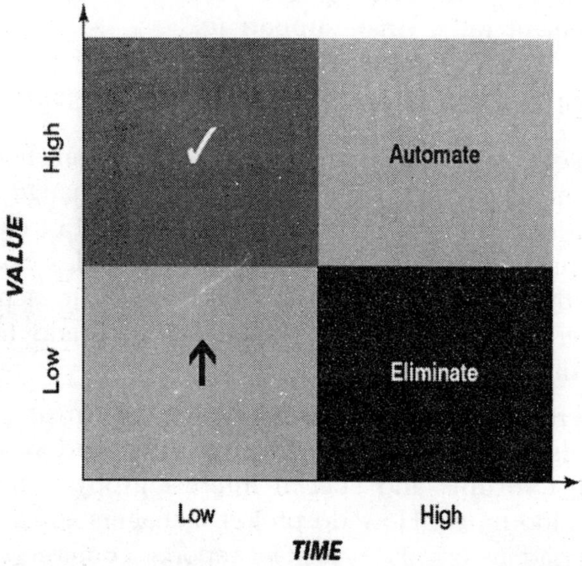

— Those falling in the bottom right-hand corner are the critical ones to address—high time but low value. Eliminate these. For example, perhaps there are meetings you don't need to attend or some that could be delegated to a member of your team, which might also be good for their personal development.

- Those in the bottom left-hand corner pose a problem. They are not consuming much time, so are reasonably efficient, but they are not delivering a lot of value. Perhaps there is a way of improving the value of each activity. You might, for example, change the agenda on a weekly operational update meeting to include asking the team to come up with at least one new idea for improvement. They add little value to the project and if dealt with straight away take little time; however, if you leave the filing and sorting of reports to build up, they will consume a disproportionate amount of time.
- Activities in the top left-hand box are already efficient and of high value. Perhaps they are already automated, so leave them until your next review. These could include, for example, the communication of tasks and updating jobs. If you have a communications process in hand then this will be automatic, but without it the project simply cannot go ahead.
- In the top right-hand box are activities such as the origination and initial thinking and planning of projects. It can take a lot of time to initiate projects in the right manner, so these activities are by definition important—high value. Although you do not want to get rid of these activities, you do need to find a more efficient way of doing them. For example, it may be that the monthly meeting you have with a regional distributor could be managed using video conferencing.

Think carefully about your overall time management: be aware of how you use your time and constantly look to find ways of improving this.

Once you have conducted a time-value assessment, you will be more conscious of this need. Don't forget that tend to do those things that enjoy and put off what is less fun. If you're serious about putting technology to the best possible use then try to overcome this psychological bias and look at the use of your time as objectively as you can. If you do not manage your time well, you will find it difficult to manage the project in addition to your other job-related activities.

When invited to meetings, constantly ask the question 'Why?' What value will the meeting give you, or what value will you give to it? If there is no obvious answer, then decline the invitation or delegate. Try a more targeted agenda or do more preparation before the meeting to reduce the meeting duration itself. The key is to remove unnecessary tasks and activities before looking for opportunities to automate: that way you avoid putting IT and other resources into something that has little or no value.

Finally, encourage your team to carry out the same exercise so that when you are deciding on various options for automation you are aiming to increase the overall effectiveness of the team, not just yourself.

TECHNOLOGY APPLICATIONS

Think carefully about how you will use technology and ensure it links back to what you are seeking to achieve. Perhaps the starting point is to look at your overall project management framework for opportunities to make each element quicker, simpler and possibly more fun. It could be that the technology might aid reporting, or planning, or even implementation. In opinion, it is very rare that technology helps with all three. Facilitation of learning, however, can be greatly enhanced through IT Anything that aids in the learning process—before, during and after a project—must be worthwhile. Some aspects of the framework will lend themselves to the use of technologies, whereas some of the softer areas, such as leadership and culture, will offer fewer opportunities or, if poorly applied, may even weaken your position as project manager.

You can also choose to use all kinds of project management software, ranging in sophistication from the simple use of Microsoft Excel to produce Gantt charts through to automated, enterprise-wide solutions such as Primavera.

TECHNOLOGY AWARENESS

Get into the habit of scanning for technology trends on the web or in industry journals. Look at what other people in your business are reading—particularly those you most admire. Where do they get their information? The web can easily be a distraction, so be wary of getting carried away with your research and straying into 'surfing' rather than specific research.

However, be aware that there is a lot of information available, and there are new technologies coming along all the time. Investigate the technology, but ask the 'So what?' question—is this relevant to team and to me, and how will it impact performance? Choose wisely—use the V-SAFE criteria as a test: does the technology add value, is it suitable, acceptable and feasible, and will it give enduring benefits? Does it provide value for money and does it link to other systems currently in place? Check those criteria before making a Go/No Go/Wait decision.

Tools Supporting Sustainable Project Management

Recognize that the development of technologies is moving so quickly that the list of what is available to you will never be static. Use the following list as a challenge to what is possible, but remember that it is a snapshot of what is happening at a point in time. The key is to get into the habit of constantly scanning this field in search of ideas for improving the effectiveness and efficiency of your project management framework.

Project management and the internet

The internet has a myriad of sites where 'Gantt heads' (those into project management on the internet) can go for free downloads, support or forums. It is an excellent tool. However, like a library where the covers from all the books have been removed, it may take some time to find what you want and what is useful. Professional bodies in the area of project management, such as the Association of Project Managers (APM) and the Project Management Institute (PMI), are excellent portals where you can go for advice, get in contact with others and find links to third-party sites.

Pros: It provides a rich source of information on a variety of project-related topics. The information is often free and you can get hold of it very fast. The internet can provide a wealth of information about tools, software, systems and case studies in a matter of minutes where previously it would have taken weeks. It also encourages creativity, as noted by US journalist Franklin P. Adams: 'I find that a great part of the information have was acquired by looking up something and finding something else on the way'.

Cons: Most of the information contains a degree of bias. After all, someone has produced it for their own purposes. It is also typically unstructured, in that a search on a topic will yield lots of results but the information on each site will be laid out in a different style. Some people call it a repository of several trillion words (and growing); the trouble is locating the 25 words you really need.

Success factors: Beware of information overload, and if new information is of critical importance then validate the information before drawing your conclusions using other sources. A neat rule of thumb is the one that journalists use—only publish a 'fact' if you have got at least two reliable sources. There are many useful sites but the best practitioners of all things 'internet' create their own collection of 'favourites'. Create a list of sites that have something specific for you to use. Subdivide them into categories, such as software, forums, research, project management methods, case studies, professional bodies (i.e. APM, PMI), etc.

Spreadsheet Software

The most basic of office tools can have a dramatic effect on the management of projects. Commonly purchased products that help in many other areas of business can have specific relevance to project management. In particular, the spreadsheet, although designed for managing numbers, can help the project manager in many ways, such as planning tasks in the Work Breakdown Structure (WBS).

Pros: Most organizations have spreadsheet software installed in their businesses. They are excellent for the creation of basic Gantt charts; in fact a simple spreadsheet is many new project managers' first experience of Gantt charts and their creation. Spreadsheets are also very useful for creating a WBS - essentially a list of tasks to do, subdivided into their constituent parts.

Cons: The spreadsheet is not specifically built for project management and therefore is somewhat limited in its scope. In experience, as soon as a project manager starts to try to manage two or more projects, competing for the same resources, on a single spreadsheet application, the complexity increases. Spreadsheets are often referred to as 'flat files' (i.e. it not a database), which means that they are fine for single projects but not so useful when you have multiple projects and want to share and extract data between them—making modifications to the spreadsheet then becomes time consuming and difficult.

Success factors: In a frequently changing project it becomes a real chore to have to 'cut and paste' new tasks into a spreadsheet; or, if members change the format of the spreadsheet to adapt to their specific needs, then merging them back together into a master task list becomes near impossible. The success factor is therefore simplicity. Remember that the more complex your project and project management environment, the more complex your needs. The more projects you manage and the greater the need to share information between them, the more likely it is that a simple spreadsheet will not meet your requirements and you will rapidly cross over from being aided by software to being restricted by it.

Word-processing

These are probably the most common and widespread of applications—even though they may not seem like project management tools. The most effective project managers are those who harness common technologies, such as Microsoft Word, and make them work for them. Turning out project-specific templates using Word can quickly save you time.

Pros: If the overall need is to communicate such things as project charters and/or objectives then a word-processing application is perfect for your needs. With a little more effort, templates can be created and before you know it you have a 'home grown' methodology driving your projects. A template will force a certain method and go some way to ensuring a certain standard of compliance.

Cons: While useful in communicating objectives and concepts, word-processing applications do little in the planning and implementation stages of project management. That's not to say that a project manager will not find such applications valuable, but they are not specialist in nature and have limited usefulness in certain areas of project management.

Success factors: Use word-processing applications to communicate with team members about objectives and basic timelines, in order to build more effective teams. Try to create templates and forms that can be reused on subsequent projects. These will not only save you time but will also start to create a standard to which others can work.

Project management software

Project management software applications (such as Microsoft Project, Primavera, WBS Tracker, etc.) are used to scope, plan, monitor and control the implementation of projects using recognized project management techniques. They provide a structured approach to managing complex projects and are fit-for-purpose in that they are designed for project management.

Pros: Project management software provides a very effective way of planning project activities, communicating objectives, allocating tasks, scheduling activities and resources, and monitoring progress. Simple outputs can also provide clear reports for all stakeholders. Web-based applications used across an organization also provide a means for managing the portfolio of projects as a whole, as opposed to managing individual projects in isolation. Generally IT departments are happy to give permission to use web-based tools, as they are easy to manage and require no downloads or physical inputs to their systems.

Cons: Most project management tools are too complex for the simpler projects. In addition, some of the most popular and well-known project tools are so over-engineered as to make them virtually unusable for all but the most specialist and professionally qualified of project managers. They tend to focus on detailed task and resource management as opposed to the typical success factors, such as having clear objectives, an effective stakeholder management process and a simple risk register. Some applications can be prohibitively expensive and IT departments generally dislike having to install and support specialist software.

Success factors: Even with all-encompassing project management software, there are risks to the novice project manager. A good starting point is to understand your needs as a project manager and the requirements of those around you. Look for a simple and easy-to-use web-based software product that meets your specific needs. Then ensure that you and key stakeholders know how to use it. For example, if your need is for project reporting, then find a tool that does that for you; if your requirement is for resource planning and scheduling, then find a tool that does that instead. Finally, don't forget that project management is as much about setting the vision and leading the team as producing impressive, if esoteric, charts and diagrams.

Video conferencing

Video conferencing allows people to communicate with both voice and video even if the other person is located elsewhere in the world—rather like having a telephone converzation with someone and being able to see them at the same time. This technology has been around for a long time, but with increased internet speeds and improved flat-screen displays, it is getting cheaper and better all the time.

Pros: The obvious advantage is that it cuts down on travel, thereby reducing costs and freeing up your time. This will have the greatest impact on companies that have high levels of spending on international flights, but it also has the potential to dramatically reduce domestic travel costs. Some systems will also tell you when the other person is available, and personal desktop-based systems are convenient and very easy to use.

Cons: Setting up video conferencing facilities within a company can be expensive, and many systems just do not offer the quality required for effective communications. They are often very impersonal, and so even when the quality of the signal is good, it does not provide personal contact and can be ineffective in, for example, sales situations.

Success factors: Investigate internet-based technologies and consider using a standard version in a pilot situation, i.e. within a small team, in order to work out whether this technology is appropriate and, if so, how you want to use it. You will need to establish management routines in terms of what to use and when to make it effective. However, in experience, video conferencing is still a poor substitute for a face-to-face meeting at a crucial part of a project. A project kick-off meeting, for instance, is a chance to motivate and inspire which can't really be done over a phone line.

Email

Electronic mail allows members of a project team to communicate via their computers. This has become the standard form of communication across and within businesses and is a key tool for effective communications.

Pros: Most organizations already have email systems, with many being free of charge. Furthermore, even though the systems are complex, most people have such a high level of familiarity that they are comfortable using them. Email systems have also become an ersatz filing system for keeping messages and reports and as such many project managers have an email filing system specifically designed for their projects.

Cons: Unfortunately, most email systems are open to a certain amount of abuse, and suffer from two issues. First, there may be a tendency to copy people in unnecessarily to keep them informed—becoming internal junk mail. Alternatively, it is easy to communicate one-on-one without including other key stakeholders in the discussion. In addition, email can stifle personal interaction: while working in a software company in the 1990s Simon found it odd that programmers and developers, working on the same project, would do *all* their communication via email and even have debates about detailed issues online—while all seated in the same room! Remember, too, that communications between members of the team often contain useful insights and lessons learned, but unless you take action to file emails, these tend to get lost on completion of the project.

Success factors: Use email selectively to direct members of the team and to communicate with key stakeholders. Set up distribution lists for certain members of the project team or stakeholders to make communication in projects simpler. However, use alternative tools for managing the projects, and specifically for capturing the vital lessons learned. Success is in realizing that email is for communication—and little else.

Blogs and forums

These are special websites that allow people to log in and discuss ideas relating to a specific topic in the form of a discussion thread, where the most recent comments are displayed first. Blogs may be created on the internet or on the company intranet and provide a place where groups of people that work together can share ideas. These groups are now often known as Communities of Practice (CoPs).

Pros: They provide a more open form of discussion than emails, as the discussion is open for others to see and is captured for future reference by other teams. Blogs work particularly well where they are focused on a specific topic—sometimes referred to as Special Interest Groups (SIGs).

Cons: Unless there is a clear reason for going to the blog, many people just don't bother, so a team leader has to encourage a team to use it and build it into their normal processes. Blogs often work best for IT teams, where they already have a culture of sharing insights and expertise, but may not work so well with other teams or departments.

Success factors: Consider carefully whether you would use a blog, and if so how? What would make it exciting and worthwhile enough to make it work within the project management community, when most people will have other commitments to focus on? Perhaps find a small team that would be interested in piloting a blog on a specific topic and see how they get on. Think about rolling out successful blogs within the organization to a wider audience -blogs seem to gain a momentum of their own for the most trivial of reasons. This might increase the interest in projects and project management generally within the organization.

Digital dashboard

A digital dashboard is a term that refers to the presentation of performance data on a computer screen—whether the manager's PC or via an LCD projector in a meeting. The senior member of the project board defines the information displayed on a project dashboard.

Pros: If set up correctly they provide an instant update on progress every time a member of the team logs in to their PC—'pushing' relevant data directly to the person with the greatest level of interest or need.

Cons: They can be costly to setup, as the underlying data typically needs to be pulled from other databases and put into a format that makes it presentable. Too often the data is not relevant to the individual user and may not be up-to-date. Digital dashboards can also radically change the culture of an organization that is used to lengthy meetings and having plenty of time to prepare reports. Such radical change can be upsetting for some managers.

Success factors: Investigate the pros and cons of creating a project dashboard for your business—what would it look like, what information would you want it to present and how would it support your project management framework? Once setup, make sure that it reflects the different needs of the different stakeholders that will be using it. If meetings are problematic, then these tools can be very helpful and the benefits across the business in reducing administration can be immense.

Lessons-learned database

A central repository of the lessons learned from previous project initiatives. It captures basic information about the project, the management, decisions made, the risks and the teams involved. It will ideally also present a 'story' of what was done and why, what the outcome was (good or bad) and perhaps what the team would do differently next time.

Pros: It is enormously valuable to the business as a means of capturing insights from individuals and teams while they remember and before they move on to new projects or jobs—or worse still leave the business.

Without active use of a lessons-learned database, organizations often repeat mistakes in terms of selecting bad ideas or implementing new ideas badly. The database should inform the next project you get involved with and colour your judgement appropriately.

Cons: Teams often don't invest the time to stop, think and learn, let alone capture the ideas for future reuse by others. Towards the end of the project many members of the team will have moved on to other commitments and they often just don't have the time. Even when insights are captured, people often don't believe that others will bother to look at them, so they are often unstructured and of little value.

Success factors: Make capturing of insights part of weekly review meetings with the team, and ensure they are captured and classified in a central, easily accessible database. Don't wait to the end of the project to do this or it will never be done. To bring the database to life, make sure that future teams are encouraged to review the database during the initial idea evaluation and project planning phases. Project directors and sponsors should, in opinion, prevent formal closure of projects until the lessons-learned database has been completed.

Keeping Equilibrium

Now stop. Before going out and investing in the latest and greatest remember that technology is just an enabler. Success will ultimately depend on your ability to lead others, your behaviours and how you interact with others.

Be wary of being drawn into new technologies too quickly—let someone else make the mistakes, but then learn quickly. Finally, if you do decide to introduce new systems to your team, think carefully about the possible risks—what could go wrong?

PROJECT IMPROVIZATIONS

There is a view that the management of project-based work is moving away from the traditional paradigm of 'plan, then execute the contents of the plan' to something rather more organic and less mechanistic. Specifically, there is a realization on the part of project and other managers that all work is different, being affected by constantly evolving and changing external influences and the dynamics of an increasingly turbulent organizational environment.

Essentially, adherents and exponents of project-based work are waking up to the idea that organizations are complex, adaptive environments, where the routines and frameworks that were applied 'last time' may not suffice to solve or resolve the issues encountered in the current project. Competent and/or progressive project managers are therefore improvizing' in order to meet current requirements.

Improvization has been defined in a number of ways, including 'the conception of action as it unfolds, by an organization and/or its members drawing on available material, cognitive, affective and social resources'. The inference here is that deciding what to do and doing it are almost simultaneous, and in reality, experienced improvisers draw on a personal library of improvizational interventions that have worked before in other instances and amend them to fit new circumstances.

Many of the ideas that underpin improvizational work come from literature on organizational 'sense-making' and in the latter part of the 1990s the components of improvizational working were identified. Essentially, the first three key elements are: creativity, involving an element of lateral thinking to devise a resolution; intuition, in that often action is based on a 'gut feeling' for what will work in a particular situation

and bricolage, a lesser-known element that basically involves 'doing the best job you can with the resources you have at hand'. Bricolage is important because project managers do not tend to have time to mobilise additional resources when conceiving and executing actions contemporaneously.

Four additional components have since been developed. These are adaption, defined as the adjustment of a routine or action to new or different conditions; compression, usually involving simplification or shortening of steps to save time; innovation, requiring deviation from existing practices or knowledge; and learning, which triggers or informs a systematic change in future behaviours.

Essentially, project managers combine these elements to respond to unplanned occurrences within projects, and experienced improvisers are adept at resolving ambiguities in this way. Organizations need to devise a framework within which improvization can happen, and that framework can be relaxed or loosened as managers develop trust in improvizing employees. There is a requirement to dismantle overtly controlling management styles, in order to allow employees the time and space to try new ways of achieving their allotted tasks.

Thus improvization is an extension of the trend towards the relaxation of control within modern organizations, allowing access to the tacitly held knowledge of experienced managers.

4

STRATEGIES FOR MANAGING CHANGE

Dor most organizations, change is inevitable. Because of this, you'll most likely be involved in managing a change project at some point—be it a simple change to the way your team deals with customer complaints, or a major change in organizational policy or strategy.

When you manage change effectively, you can move your organization into the new "business as usual" state swiftly, and you'll find that other people are quick to accept change. This means that your team and organization experiences the minimum disruption, and projects succeed, rather than stall and fail.

Managing change is a challenging and important task. If you apply a process and use a variety of tools, you can design a change plan that people will accept and work hard to implement, leading to less disruption to your team and organization.

Because change doesn't happen in isolation, you must understand how change works, then broaden your thinking, brainstorm potential impacts, and maintain open communication with people.

Change management doesn't end as soon as the change is implemented. Make sure you continue to communicate achievements, and ensure that people have the skills needed to do what they are being asked to do. By taking an extensive and proactive approach to your change projects, you'll enjoy greater success, and you'll be able to build on that success for many other change projects in the future.

There are four key areas of successful change management. They are:

1. Understanding change.
2. Planning change.
3. Managing resistance to change.
4. Implementing change.

By addressing each area, you'll be better prepared to plan and implement successful change projects. We'll look at each area separately, and provide links to more in-depth resources that you can use in the change management process.

UNDERSTANDING CHANGE

Before you manage a project that involves changing the way that people work, you must first understand how people react to change. Then you'll be in a better position to plan proactively for the stages of change, and for the effect that change has on your organization.

The Change Curve theory describes people's reactions to each stage of change. These reactions can range from "shock and denial," when business as usual is first disrupted, to "acceptance" and "commitment," as the change is implemented.

Many people need time to adjust and accept the change. So levels of performance may fall as they learn how to use new systems and processes. Lewin's Change Management Model of "Unfreeze-Change-Refreeze" highlights why you need to build sufficient time into the process for people to adjust, and provide a lot of consultation with those affected by the change.

Theories about how organizations change draw on many disciplines, from psychology and behavioral science, through to engineering and systems thinking. The underlying principle is that change does not happen in isolation—it impacts the whole organization (system) around it, and all the people touched by it.

In order to manage change successfully, it is therefore necessary to attend to the wider impacts of the changes. As well as considering the tangible impacts of change, it's important to consider the personal impact on those affected, and their journey towards working and behaving in new ways to support the change.

Change management is a very broad field, and change management approaches vary widely, from organization to organization and from project to project. Many organizations and consultants subscribe to formal change management methodologies. These provide toolkits, checklists and outline plans of what needs to be done to manage changes successfully.

When you are tasked with "managing change" (irrespective of whether or not you subscribe to a particular change management approach), the first question to consider is what change management actually means in your situation. Change management focuses on people, and is about ensuring change is thoroughly, smoothly and lastingly implemented. And to know what that means exactly in your situation, you must dig down further to define your specific change management objectives.

Typically, these will cover:

- *Sponsorship*: Ensuring there is active sponsorship for the change at a senior executive level within the organization, and engaging this sponsorship to achieve the desired results.

- *Buy-in*: Gaining buy-in for the changes from those involved and affected, directly or indirectly.
- *Involvement*: Involving the right people in the design and implementation of changes, to make sure the right changes are made.
- *Impact*: Assessing and addressing how the changes will affect people.
- *Communication*: Telling everyone who's affected about the changes.
- *Readiness*: Getting people ready to adapt to the changes, by ensuring they have the right information, training and help.

When you are defining your change management objectives and activities, it's very important to coordinate closely with others: project managers, managers in the business, and the HR department. Ask "who's responsible?" For example, who's responsible for identifying change agents? Defining the re-training plan? Changing job descriptions and employment contracts? And so on.

As every change is different, responsibilities will vary depending on how the change activities and project are organized. Only when you know who's responsible and how things are organized in your situation will you know what's within your change management scope, and how you'll be working with other people to bring about the change.

PLANNING CHANGE

The quote that "If you fail to plan, you're planning to fail" is as true with change management as it is with anything else. As ever, thorough preparation is the key to successful planning.

As part of this, conducting an Impact Analysis will help you understand the possible positive and negative consequences of change, so that you can develop contingency plans to deal with any issues that may arise.

The Burke-Litwin Change Model will help you identify every potential area of impact. It maps out the interrelated complexity of organizational structures, and helps you track how your proposed change project will affect other areas of your organization. Leavitt's Diamond is another tool that analyses how change can impact your organization. It looks at the four major components of an organization—structure, technology, people, and tasks—and helps you think about how changes to these components can affect each other.

Once you have considered the change management objectives and scope, you'll also need to consider the specific tasks. Again, the range of possible change management activities is broad. It's a question of working out what will best help you meet the change management challenge in hand, as you have defined it in your objectives and scope, and how to work along side other people's and projects' activities and responsibilities.

The essence of this is to identify the tasks that are necessary if you're going to give change the greatest chance of success.

Coming from this, the activities involved in managing change can include:

— Ensuring there is clear expression of the reasons for change, and helping the sponsor communicate this.
— Identifying "change agents" and other people who need to be involved in specific change activities, such as design, testing, and problem solving, and who can then act as ambassadors for change.

- Assessing all the stakeholders and defining the nature of sponsorship, involvement and communication that will be required.
- Planning the involvement and project activities of the change sponsor(s).
- Planning how and when the changes will be communicated, and organizing and/or delivering the communications messages.
- Assessing the impact of the changes on people and the organization's structure.
- Planning activities needed to address the impacts of the change.
- Ensuring that people involved and affected by the change understand the process change.
- Making sure those involved or affected have help and support during times of uncertainty and upheaval.
- Assessing training needs driven by the change, and planning when and how this will be implemented.
- Identifying and agreeing the success indicators for change, and ensure they are regularly measured and reported on.

Remember, these are just some typical change management activities. Others may be required in your specific situation. Equally, some of the above may not be within your remit, so plan carefully, and coordinate with other people involved.

MANAGING RESISTANCE TO CHANGE

Many people are uncomfortable with change. So a large part of managing change is overcoming resistance, and promote acceptance and belief in the change.

You can overcome this resistance by communicating effectively. Talk about why change is necessary, and share your vision of change with everyone. This includes talking to all stakeholders and getting their support early in the process. These early discussions can help you assess the various barriers to change, and then plan how to manage stakeholders as you move the project forward.For people to be motivated to change, they must be dissatisfied with the current situation, and must think that the proposed solution is desirable and practical. Use this equation to assess readiness for change, so you can ensure that a change is actually needed, and that your planned changes will result in significant benefits.

How does your organization approach change? Do people respond with a sharp intake of breath when they first hear about a proposed new initiative, and then go on to try and find reasons why it won't work? Or do they react by saying things like "What a great idea, and we could also.." In other words, is your corporate culture against or for change?

Corporate culture is a powerful force that runs through every organization. It is defined as the attitudes, experiences, beliefs, and values that operate within an organization. And these undercurrents define people's behaviour, and how a company gets things done, in either positive or negative ways.

When successful change is the desired outcome, these cultural factors play a very important role. If an organization has had a negative experience of change in the past, then change will be that much more difficult the next time around. Likewise, if the prevailing attitude is represented by the saying, "If it ain't broke, don't fix it", then making any kind of change will be met with that much more resistance.

Effecting change is difficult at the best of times. When you encounter resistance due to cultural elements, it can be even more frustrating. This is because the very elements of corporate culture are so difficult to see and pinpoint.

It is worth remembering here that while culture issues can present barriers to change, they can also support change and goal achievement. To overcome cultural barriers the best way to start is to look at the characteristics of a high performance culture. Once you know what you "should" be doing or promoting, it is easier to make a plan to revamp your current situation.

DREC Curve

To a large degree change management, for that is what this really is, is about overcoming resistance and people's fears and objections to your plan. To that end many successful clients have adopted the DREC curve as a means of understanding people's attitudes to changes. DREC stands for the four 'emotions' you may come across while introducing change—for example, a new project management framework:

- Denial
- Resistance
- Exploration
- Commitment.

In figure 1, the statements illustrate fictional reactions to an event, but what is important is the curve through the four quadrants. How you manage these reactions is crucial to the smooth implementation of change. So, in the example of a new project management framework, you could try the following strategies:

- *Denial*. Initially the team might say, 'We don't need a project management framework' or 'This framework will be a waste of time and effort'. At this stage many comments are emotional and not rational and are borne out of fear of change. Many clients inform us that it is often best to allow colleagues to get their fears off their chest and allow them a 'rant' at this stage. Your role as owner of the project is to get through this stage as quickly and as painlessly as possible, *not* to hit their denial head on, which may only prolong matters and create opponents.

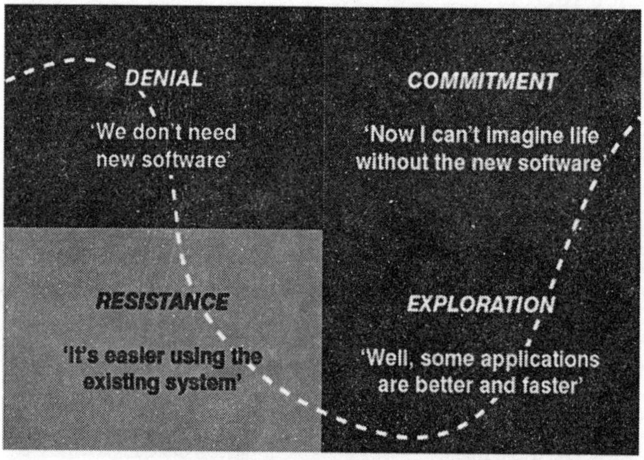

Figure 1. DREC Curve

— *Resistance.* At this stage there may be a tacit acceptance of the need for change, but its relevance may be limited to the individual in question. The framework may be useful to you but not for department' or 'Well, you'll have to do it in your time and with your resources, as it's not needed by team' are the statements you may hear at this stage. Your role as the leader of the initiative is to get resisters to understand the benefits of your approach and to get them at least to explore certain scenarios and opportunities.

- *Exploration.* Your role at this stage is to expand the areas in which the resister might find your project management framework useful, albeit on a limited scale. It may be about selling the benefits of the framework and showing how it might solve problems for the individual. It may be about getting them to use the framework on a limited basis or piloting it for a limited time only—a taster with no commitment at this stage.
- *Commitment.* Ultimately this is where are trying to get people to—an acceptance that your framework is fundamental to the running of projects within the business, which in fact they couldn't do without it. However, don't look for praise or reward, as this may be another uphill struggle. Your reward should be the implementation of your initiative.

People using the DREC curve talk about the leader's role being that of getting people to the fourth quadrant as quickly and as painlessly as possible, but having to go through the three previous quadrants first. There is no jumping quadrants—no easy jump from denial to commitment. Once you understand how resistance to change manifests itself, you can focus on the process by which you implement your integrated project management framework.

IMPLEMENTING CHANGE

When you implement change, further communication is crucial—you'll almost certainly have problems at some point, and if you aren't regularly talking about the plan and communicating your successes, people may go back to old ways of doing things. The following three steps are crucial for successful implementation:

1. Create short-term wins.
2. Build on the change.
3. Anchor the changes in corporate culture.

So aim for a few early achievements to showcase the benefits of the change. This can help keep motivation and enthusiasm for the change high.

Then highlight building on the change you started, and work toward making it part of the organizational culture. This can separate "good" change management from "great" change management. Good change management is when you are satisfied when you meet your initial objective. Great change management is when you keep adjusting your target for continuous improvement—you aren't afraid to keep changing things, because you're confident in your ability to keep making progress

Ensuring Success

How do you keep track of what is going on? Once your project has been launched, your primary role as the project manager is to keep it on track. Remember the old military adage, 'No plan survives contact with the enemy'—which means that simply putting a plan together, no matter how carefully constructed, will not ensure that it will run smoothly or even at all. You need to create a feedback system, a mechanism by which you can manage and balance three distinct elements:

- plans-timings and tasks
- people—stakeholders and allocated tasks
- performance -the objectives, goal and quality of the project.

A simple process to use is the plan-do-check-act cycle—abbreviated to PDCA. It is a continuous improvement approach to monitoring and managing a project or a team (Figure 2).

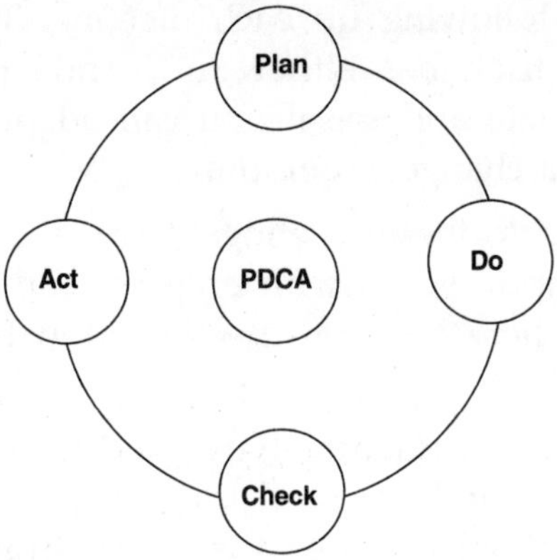

Figure 2

- Plan your projects and deliverables—the Gantt chart, critical path analysis and Work Breakdown Structure (WBS) are visible representations of this step.
- Do the tasks, using the necessary resources.
- Check all the projects' progress at the milestones or gates you have built into the plan. These are the points at which issues or problems may emerge and may require an amendment to plans. Your effort should go into managing the changes and issues rather than the actual checking progress, so the more you can automate or delegate the checking of activities, the better.
- Act upon the issues raised in the checking step. This will involve new decisions, actions or re-planning—all with the aim of bringing projects back on track to meet their objectives and goals.

As part of the drive to simplify the checking process you should be looking to setup a regular schedule of meetings, in addition to the formal end of stage gate meetings. To make these meetings work for you, try to ensure that you have a standard template for preparing, running and following up each meeting. Think whether your organization has either an agenda template or a minutes template and see if you can adapt them for the needs of your change programme.

In addition to these meetings, think about briefings to keep people up to speed with progress and project issues. A distinction here between meetings and briefings:

- Formal meetings need to be planned for and factored into Gantt charts and work breakdown structures and are used to formally check progress and deal with issues that arise from monitoring performance.
- Briefings can be quick and simple five-minute updates to keep people abreast of the situation. Make a distinction between the two and plan accordingly.

Critical Success Factors

How can increase chances of implementing an effective integrated project management framework?

- Start the change programme with a 'quick win'. 'Nothing succeeds like success', so try to pick some 'low hanging fruit' in terms of easily attainable goals or objectives. This will motivate the team. Communicate these successes widely
- Get active commitment from the senior management team within your business. The change programme is an internally facing project and therefore you should get some internal support. The higher the better.
- Develop a system or process to help with reporting, monitoring and communicating. These functions are common to all types of project. Get these in order and your administrative burden as a project manager will reduce.

– Focus on high-value objectives that fit the current business need. You know there is a need for an integrated project management framework, but what specific business issues can be resolved? These should be your focus.
– Reward people for sharing ideas and ways of doing things. As change programmes are internally focused (as opposed to being client focused), look for ideas from all staff and reward those who come up with good ideas, irrespective of whether they are in your project team or not.
– Use the change programme as a way of assessing the performance of your project teams. This will help you to select those to involve in important client-facing projects.
– Develop skills to improve the quality of the work people do in project management. This will improve the overall effectiveness and efficiency of the project management framework/ infrastructure.
– Communicate, communicate, communicate. Always and often.
– Evaluate progress and assess performance in a regular, standard way.
– Learn from your failures as well as your successes. Keep a 'lessons-learned' log to help the project team and to improve every project you do.

LEADING THE CHANGE

Remember that it is people who run projects, not systems, software or processes. To that end you need to ensure that you are flexible and responsive to the needs of stakeholders and the project team. Think about your style of management and how much leeway you give your teams in terms of making decisions and taking action.

Often this style is reflected in the detail that project managers insist upon in the Work Breakdown Structure (WBS). If you break down the project into too much detail you run the following risks:

- You make a rod for your own back. Ultimately, you, as the project manager, will have to ensure that all elements on the WBS are done. So the more elements you put in, the more you will have to check.
- Too much detail reduces flexibility for your team. If they already have an efficient way of doing a task on the WBS, but you have mandated more detail on *how* they should do it, then you waste this opportunity and skill. Make sure you only tell people *what* to do and not *how* to do it: one is content and the other is stylistic.
- Being too prescriptive demotivates people. If you trust your staff to do a job well, then don't do the project management equivalent of standing over them!

However, there are also risks in not giving enough guidance within the WBS:

- Not enough detail for inexperienced team members can lead to indecision and falling behind in project schedules.
- Enthusiastic team members can do too much of the wrong thing or not enough of the right thing if the WBS and guidelines are too vague.
- You run the risk of not meeting the project objectives if the planned tasks are too 'high level'.

Ultimately it is a balance of how much detail you as a manager insist upon, and this will be reflected in how loose or tight your management style is. The right level will come with experience and also your knowledge of the people you are working with.

As a leader, don't get bogged down by using project tools and techniques at the expense of moving the project forward. Use cértain techniques if they add value but be flexible and always look for shortcuts and better ways of doing things. Often your team can be the best source of these ideas, so tap into their creative side as often as you can and don't be restricted by sticking to processes too rigidly.

Project management is easy. Deliver what people need when they want it. Achieve this by questioning what they think they want, agreeing a scope and how to deliver it, applying lessons of handling the uncertainties organizing the resources needed, checking that the client is willing and ready to do what they need to do, living with them to see that they do it, preparing the customer for what they get, and always adjusting to what happens.

So why is project management largely 'fire-fighting'—having to find means of overcoming immediate threats to the delivery of the intended project which could have been anticipated? Questioning people on projects in the construction, manufacturing, process and service industries in North West Europe reveals that they suffer many threats to delivering projects successfully.

The greatest threats stem from problems of roles, communications, leadership, supervision, teamwork and trust—what can be classed as *organizational* problems. Problems of *time* and *resources* are also substantial, and after them problems of *project definition, cost, contracts* and *change.* By contrast, *risk, quality* and *safety* are not seen to be major problems.

The data from different sectors of industry is remarkably similar, even with different types of employer and size of project, and over 18 years of questioning. These greatest problems thus appear to be typically characteristic of project work, at least in the Western cultures represented in this data. Over the past few decades the growth in industrial and professional attention to the needs of projects indicates much more awareness of the potential problems and how to manage them. This should have reduced the impact of the problems and increased confidence in controlling them, yet these same categories of problem persist. They remain a definition of the main tasks of project management. Although the word 'unique' is used in some definitions of what a project is, many writers observe that the life cycles of all types of project are similar. So, too, may be the problems that need to be anticipated and controlled through any project.

Most of the reported problems are due to practices within organizations—institutional habits and unwise decisions. They could therefore be avoided and fire-fighting could become redundant, or at least much reduced. The first task of project management must therefore be to look at the causes of potential problems of roles, communications, leadership, supervision, teamwork and trust. Above all, this requires skills in organizational relationships.

❖❖❖

5

HOW TO BECOME A BETTER PROJECT MANAGER?

Whether or not you hold the official title of project manager, chances are you'll be called upon to lead some sort of project at some time. From initiating a procedural change in your department to opening a branch office in a different cities, projects come in all shapes and sizes. As the complexity increases, the number of details you have to monitor also increases. However, the fundamentals of managing a project from start to finish are usually very similar. Whatever you have decided to do in terms of developing your career as a manager, to be successful you need to take control, plan and focus on the things that will really make a difference. You need to ask yourself how you get into your company's key talent pool.

Once you have successfully eased yourself into your new role and gained the trust of your boss and the team, you can start to make things happen. First, focus on your leadership style and how it needs to change to suit the new role; then focus on the team. Are they the right people and, if so, what will make them work more effectively as a project team?

At the appropriate time, you need to think about your next career move, and whether you are interested in getting to the top and becoming a company director. This is not for everyone, as the commitment, time and associated stress can be off-putting, but the sense of responsibility and leadership can be enormously rewarding.

MAKING A GOOD CAREER

The starting time period for doing a new role as the leader of a project team are probably the most critical—get them wrong and you risk failure, get them right and you will enjoy and thrive in your new role. For most people project management is a 'part-time' role. By that mean that they are asked to manage a project, or series of projects, in addition to their day-to-day function. There are also many people who are full-time project or programme management professionals, in which project management is their core discipline. If you are a person new to managing projects, as well as coping with your usual activities how are you going to make a difference within the starting time period?

Let us answer that by asking another question—what happens if you don't make any progress within the first two months or, even worse, make progress in the wrong direction? If your answer to that question is that such a situation is unthinkable, you now need to ask yourself the following:

- What should I do?
- Where should I focus effort and attention?
- What must avoid at all costs?

As a new good manager, you will need to understand key facts, build relationships and develop mechanisms for monitoring and control—establishing simple but effective processes for understanding how things are progressing and what line managers are focusing on. Modern technologies can simplify these tasks, but there is no substitute for getting to know people and forming good working relationships with individuals and creating a supportive culture.

The best example of this we've come across was a new sales director for a telecoms company in the UK. In a quiet moment asked him when he had taken up smoking a pipe. 'I haven't,' he said, 'I just use it as an excuse or prop to allow to get in with the smokers on the fire escape.' When asked why he wanted to do that, he stated that the smokers were often the best-informed people in the organization because they spent their smoke breaks discussing business issues and rumours across almost all the functions. He had created an informal network from the tobacco addicts on the fire escape. siness with them.

In your new role, you may need to choose and use differing leadership styles based on specific project situations. Making the right choice is a skill that will come with the experience. Many people new to project management believe that because they have been given the role of 'project manager' and have a copy of the latest scheduling software, people will do their bidding automatically. Actually, people make projects successful, not software or systems. Developing working relationships is a vital first step in your 'career'—either part-time or full-time'—in project management.

CHANGING ROLES

Whenever you start a new role or job, whether within your existing business or joining a new company, you have an opportunity to make a positive impression on others. However, remember that you will only get one chance to make a first impression—get the first few months wrong and it could impact your relationships with others for a very long time. While working in the NHS, Simon came across a project manager with the nickname 'Shouty'. He asked whether the nickname was supposed to be ironic, as the manager seemed to be the most placid and calm of all managers in the NHS Trust. Simon was told that when Shouty had first joined the Trust, he had a habit of barking orders to people. In fact, Shouty hadn't barked an order to people in over the years, but first impressions stick, if only in a nickname.

During a period of transition, the team you are joining will normally have few preconceptions of you. People may have an open mind and be willing to try new ideas: they give you the benefit of the doubt. The consultants often say exactly the same things as some of the internal managers, but as outsiders their views are respected and acted upon. Indeed it is an accepted, though controversial, practice to bring in consultants to recommend bad news, like the closure of a department, even though the internal managers know that it has to be done. The lesson to learn from this is that if there is going to be bad news, spend time to identify it quickly so that you can announce it before you have fully bonded with your team.

The starting time is typically a period of high emotional energy when activities will often get a higher level of enthusiasm and commitment. Use this time wisely and you will gain a significant advantage.

POTENTIAL PITFALLS

While this period of transition presents opportunities to make a good impression, take care not to get it wrong. Few people recover from a bad start in a new role. You will be faced with a number of challenges to overcome:

- You will lack knowledge and expertise in your new role. This will make you vulnerable to getting decisions wrong. Being a good judge of character will help, as people will always offer suggestions to new starters and you need to decide whether to follow their advice. Ultimately, of course, you will be judged on your own decisions but look around to see whether there is someone whose judgement and assessment of other people you can trust. Take their opinions as useful input, but remember that the decisions will be yours.
- Getting in with the wrong people can limit your opportunities for future promotion. In every team there will be a mixture of people and opinions, so try to understand the office politics before you take any decision. Is the department under the microscope, expanding or readying itself for redundancies? How critical is the team to the success of the higher business unit or the company as a whole?
- There will be a lot to do in a short time and you may well feel overwhelmed by it all. Prioritise, prioritise, prioritise! There are so many hours in the day, so although you may be tempted to go in like a whirling dervish and sort everything out at once, the practical reality is you won't be able to. You need to work out what is important and make progress on those few, key issues first.
- Most effective managers rely heavily on their informal networks, but in the early stages of a new job these don't exist. Judge people by their actions rather than their words. Trust those who deliver or who have a good reputation for delivering. Try to build informal networks outside your department or team, as well as sounding boards within it. The most progressive of companies now run a mentor

programme for up-and-coming managers. A mentoring programme focuses on the individual within the current company context. It is not necessarily about skill development but helps the individual perform within the particular business environment in which they find themselves. Most senior managers are flattered to be asked for their advice and experience. Not only that—it's also good business sense.

Because people sometimes give new starters the benefit of the doubt things often seem to go well for a period of time. If you make mistakes they will forgive you because you're new to the job. This is referred to as the 'honeymoon period'. New football coaches, for example, are allowed to lose the first few games without too much criticism. However, after a period of time (the first two months), you, like the coaches, will need to perform well, meeting the expectations of key stakeholders and winning them over as supporters.

During this initial period, it is vital that you take the necessary steps to set yourself up for longer-term success. Otherwise you run the risk of, as it were, falling into the chasm—you make a good start but then people begin to see what you are doing as just another management initiative. You need not only to make initial gains and successes but also to sow the seeds for longer-term success. A trap that many new managers fall into is that the first few weeks of their new role is unlike the rest of their job, it is atypical, but they plan on the longer-term being like the short term. Plan your first two months carefully in order to set yourself up for longer-term success.

HOW TO START?

Before starting a new project or job within the area of

project and programme management, you need to do your research to find out what it will entail and what some of the potential problems are likely to be. Develop a personal to-do list of things to get ready or put in place. How will you behave differently, what knowledge will you need to gain and what new skills would be useful? Understanding these things will help to build your confidence.It is also useful, if not crucial, to identify key influencers in the project management arena, such as industry experts or your internal operations director, and start to build your reputation. Again, this is where a formal or informal mentor programme can help out.

When suggest to young managers that they need to create a plan for their first few months, get many a raised eyebrow, usually from experienced managers. 'I never needed that sort of thing' is the usual comment. However, times have changed and business has never been so unforgiving. Learning on the job means exactly that—learning from mistakes and getting better with time. Since the pace of change has never been faster, now all management gurus agree that the learning curve' is a lot steeper.

People today expect more, faster and are less forgiving. There are always some senior managers who realise that mistakes are a chance to learn and improve, but, in experience, they are few and far between. If you do find yourself working for a senior manager who is enlightened enough to help you learn from your mistakes as well as dissect your successes, then firmly hitch yourself to their coat-tails, as they are a rare breed indeed.

A ten-step plan is a great idea. In the numerous roles and jobs that have had over many years can think of many occasions where such a plan would have helped put things into some sort of perspective. Use the following suggestions to put together a plan for the first few months in your new position as a project manager.

Step 1: Get to Know Your Stakeholders

First impression influences the way a relationship develops in the first few months. Start by understanding the key stakeholders in the area in which you are working, what their roles are and how each could impact on your success. These stakeholders will typically include your boss, work colleagues, your project teams, functional heads, key opinion leaders, subject matter experts, key customers and suppliers. Knowing who they are and making a comprehensive list of them is a good starting point. If, for example, you are going to manage a project that changes how salespeople enter new sales orders, then put senior salespeople and managers on the stakeholder list, even though their actual involvement may be further down the line. You're trying to pre-empt problems here and make it more certain that you will gain acceptance of the impact that your project is going to have on other people.

Develop a communication plan that includes face-to-face discussions, to improve the support for your team from all the highly influential stakeholders. There is no substitute for face-to-face meetings. It is better to start with these meetings rather than trying to introduce your way of doing things and your suggestions from an unknown email address.

It is worthwhile assessing each stakeholder group on a power versus support matrix (Figure 1). Focus on those stakeholders who have the greatest power or influence over your work. Think hard about how you can win round those that will oppose your ideas and consider ways of using the support of your advocates. Remember that if you don't do this analysis you will be drawn into spending more time with people who agree with you and they may not be part of the power base you need. In effect you will be talking to the people in the green square of the influence/support matrix when probably you should be spending time with the people in the red area. By definition, it is people in the red area who can prevent your project succeeding.

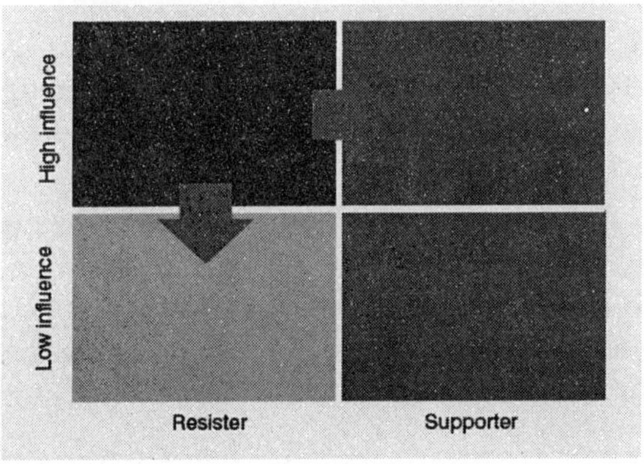

Figure 1

Step 2: Capture a Business Snapshot

You obviously need to understand the business you are working in. Get to know what the priorities are and the critical success factors for this current year.

You will need an appreciation of the overall strategy of your organization in order to validate whether projects should be included in the overall portfolio. Then develop a project that will help in the effective working of business. The test is whether you can give a confident answer to the question, 'How is your project pushing the company towards its strategic objectives and goals?'

Assess the current situation and where you think the business is. Is it a new or start-up business, or a steady-state organization in a mature market? Is it in the process of rapid growth, a business turnaround to regain profitability, or possibly even in a wind-down phase?

Your quick snapshot should also confirm what budgets and resources you already have for projects. This helps you assess the level of importance the business places on this particular activity.

Step 3: Create a Team SWOT

Critically evaluate each aspect of your project team and identify those areas that you consider to be strengths and weaknesses, and areas that reflect opportunities and threats.

Take time to share your thoughts with your boss and other key stakeholders—this will provide an opportunity to get to know them better and to start thinking about ways to address weaknesses and exploit strengths. Here's an example:

Strengths	*Weaknesses*
CEO enthusiasm for project management Clear portfolio priorities for the current year Committed project teams with sufficient budget and time	No common project process across functional teams—inefficient and ineffective Limited visibility of current initiatives at senior level Poor learning at end of projects
Opportunities	***Threats***
Cost reduction programme could be a major programme New product development process needs to be redesigned	Poor financial performance may reduce project budget

The project manager has identified weaknesses in the way initiatives are managed across the business and the level of visibility the project portfolio has at the senior management team (SMT) level. At the same time, they believe that they have great teams and the full support of the chief executive. Perhaps a project manager in this situation might seek to use the CEO's enthusiasm to introduce some sort of project process to help give the SMT visibility and control over the project portfolio.

Step 4: Secure Quick Wins

Make a list of your ideas for change as you progress, and then prioritise them in terms of impact on the business and urgency. Measure impact in terms of how each change will support a specific business imperative, or the difference it will make to overall profitability. Measure urgency in terms of specific deadlines that need to be met or windows of opportunity, such as, for example, implementing a process change during the summer holiday period.

For those changes that you consider to be a priority, identify one or two that you know you can implement quickly, within a few days, and with little risk. These are referred to as 'quick wins' and will do a lot to boost your credibility within the organization—assuming they succeed. Often it is better to get a quick win of minor importance than strive for a major gain later on. The low hanging fruit' needs to be grabbed straight away.

Think carefully about potential problems and take time to meet with the relevant stakeholders to ensure fast success. You can then communicate these quick wins in a way that builds commitment to the overall project management programme, and builds your credibility.

For example, an effective quick win might be to conduct a one-day workshop with the different operational teams across the business, and simply capture and share their respective projects. During the workshop, ask each team participant to present their approach to managing their project, and then facilitate a discussion about the benefits of creating a common approach to managing projects, prioritization and communication. In this way you will not only have built credibility among a key group of people, but you will also have started the process of creating common practices and increasing visibility of the overall project portfolio.

Step 5: Create a Vision

At the end of your first month in your new role, stop and take stock of where you are. Reflect on what you have learnt, and the key messages you have received from your boss and other key stakeholders. You should now have enough information and insights to put together your vision for at least the next year, or possibly two.

Start at the end and think about what you want to have achieved before you move on to your next role, whether it be in six months or three years. The clearer your vision of what success will look like, the more likely it is that you will achieve it. Think about how you want people to remember you after you have moved on: what will they say about you?

Then translate this vision into a team strategy or plan. This should clarify what you will do in terms of your effect on the products and services the company provides. Also decide what you're not going to do. Clarifying boundaries like this helps to focus the team and ensure that your limited project resources and budget are not spread too thinly. Then think carefully about who your customers are, whether internal or external to the business, and which are the most important. If your customers are external to the business, make sure you understand the company's marketing strategy and that your vision chimes with it.

Your vision should also clearly articulate your approach to each of the Good top ten project management elements, namely:

- project goals
- stakeholders
- workplan and timings
- issues and risks
- the team
- critical decisions
- resources and budget
- business needs
- project leadership
- communications.

Within these elements you might identify what you see as the biggest gaps and how and when each will be closed. At this stage your vision does not need to be a detailed statement, but it should provide a roadmap stating clearly what you are looking to achieve. You will of course need to take time to validate your plan with members of the team and with your boss.

As well as putting a plan in place for the team, think about the capabilities you personally need to build in order to lead the team successfully. Where there are gaps, create your own personal development plan for gaining the necessary skills or experience. Sell this to your boss to gain their approval that you should spend the time and money to plug the gaps.

Finally, at this stage you should reflect on your new role and ensure that you are able to balance your work commitments with your preferred lifestyle. There is no point in doing a great job it you burn out in the next ten months.

Step 6: Take a Break!

Even the most capable and confident managers tend to use up a lot of nervous energy when getting stuck into a new job. Spend time with each team member on a one-on-one basis and listen to their views, their aspirations and their concerns. Get to know the whole person, not just that part of them that is involved with getting their job done. Motivating and rewarding people is much easier if you know their hobbies, eccentricities and opinions. Talk to your key stakeholders and test the various elements of your project vision, updating it as you go.

In the military it is common practice to understand the role and function of each individual under your command. That is not to say that you are expected, as a manager, to do the job better or faster than your people, but at least you should understand what the individual issues are and what motivates each team member to do a good job. This approach could be applied to any work situation. It just takes effort and time. It is experience that this is time well spent and that individuals appreciate management time taken to understand them and their issues.

Pay particular attention to your boss, and get to know them better. Realizing that in large corporations your immediate boss and their boss can have a major influence on your working day, people have started to think about how they can 'manage their manager'. This is not about ingratiating yourself with your manager for personal gain—that would be a Good to getting the wrong sort of reputation—but about understanding your immediate boss's objectives and targets. Since their actions will ultimately affect you, knowing your boss well gives you another channel by which you can understand what is happening in the business and what is in the pipeline.

Make sure you get on top of your day-to-day administration and clear as much of your in-box as possible. Ensure that your email list is under control and take time to delegate non-critical tasks to members of the team as early as possible. Some people find that setting up filing systems, mobile phone records, email folders and a diary system is second nature—it happens 'automatically'—but others have to work at it.

While working in a banking corporation came across many managers who shared secretaries and PAs. The key to success, observed, is to ensure that you understand how the other manager works and come to a common style and way of working. Setup an informal 'contract' of how you will work, all three of you, for best results.

Step 7: Build your Reputation with Others

Right, back into the fray. Recognize that your new role is fundamentally different from your previous role and that in order to succeed you may need to do things differently. This is particularly important when it is your first role in management, so you will have switched from achieving results through your own efforts and expertise to achieving results through others. Remember that your personal reputation will now be dependent on the ability of the team to deliver results. Some managers find the correct plan of action counter-intuitive. They try to take the glory for good results and blame their team for the mistakes they make. The Good manager knows to do exactly the opposite: they praise the team for good results in front of senior managers and take complete responsibility for things that go wrong.

While working in a technical support call centre as customer service manager, Simon often used to bring in team members to the fortnightly management meeting to give feedback on performance and customer issues, rather than reinterpreting the information given to him and delivering it himself. After the initial panic, they were coached on their specific part of the agenda and how management wanted the data to be presented. They were shown how to distil information down into discrete chunks and not to 'tell a story'. Simon always supported them within the meeting, and management soon realised the benefit of getting information 'from the horse's mouth'.

This approach to building a team reputation with managers had some interesting results:

- The technical support department, once undervalued, came to be seen as a valuable source of customer information.
- The individuals within the department started to be valued more—in fact the meetings became a potential recruiting ground for the development and testing teams.
- Simon could now leave the more repetitive aspects of the fortnightly management meetings to others, while he focused on more pressing issues and strategic tasks.
- Individuals, once shy of giving feedback at meetings, came to see it as management 'education' and part of improving their promotion prospects; Simon saw it as succession planning; the management team saw it as just good organization.

These 'virtual teams' are often more challenging to lead, so in order to build your reputation you must be sensitive to the needs of individual members and understand what each function is trying to achieve. To get the best results, adapt how you work with them, talking in their terms.

Take time to build your network. The more senior you become, the more important your network will be to your future success. Your key contacts will initially be internal to the business, but as you become more established, look outside the business at professional bodies. Be critical in terms of how you use your time, as some of the network organizations you can join promise a lot but deliver little, but as a project manager in the business seek to identify and bring in best practices from other organizations.

All the organizations have 'special interest groups' or areas dealing with project management and skill development for project managers in their specialist fields. These are formal organizations and associations, but also gain much experience and learning from the less formal, personal networking groups and clubs to which both belong. Neither of us joined formal organizations or informal groups specifically to improve individual learning or standing in project management; joined to meet other people and understand whether they had the same issues. However, the long-term benefits of such groups easily outweigh the odd evening having to listen to others rather than being at home. You just need to decide which groups and events will offer the most.

Step 8: Conduct Your First Project Reviews

Your quick wins will have given you a feel for what is possible, but more importantly they will have helped to build your reputation as someone who gets things done. You will also have established relationships with key people across the business.

Now is the time to hold your first structured review of the project or projects, aimed at delivering real value to the business. Focus on a current business issue or key success factor and get the right people involved. Plan the review thoroughly and think about all the things that could take it off track. You may want to have the individuals present a brief overview of their parts of the project(s), highlighting the overall business benefits and demonstrating the link to the organization's strategy and why they should receive the necessary resources to achieve all the project objectives.

The project review can be a very formal process and as a result many issues may be uncovered. It may generate more work for you and perhaps some uncomfortable decisions, but that is what it is for—not just to check progress.

Step 9: Reflect and Learn

Now stop and review where you are. Take an hour or so at the start to sit back and reflect on what has gone well, what has gone badly, and why. Go back to your original plan or to-do list and check off the items you have delivered against, and then critically review areas where you failed to meet expectations.

Meet with your boss and ask for a formal review of your progress. Many bosses are not very good at doing formal performance reviews, but nevertheless it is an essential part of continuous improvement. Then meet with your other stakeholders and get their input into what has gone well and what they would like to see changed. You may need to amend the way that you review the projects that come under your area of responsibility—how you monitor and control the progress of the various projects and how you can bring specific projects back on track.

Step 10: Develop Your Plan

Over the last nine steps you have built your reputation and credibility as a project (or even programme) manager, you have developed important relationships with influential stakeholders and your confidence has grown. You will by now have an opinion on what you want to achieve, based on facts and the advice of experts around the business. Now is the time to develop your two-year plan. The project reviews may substantially contribute to this as well.

Start by reflecting on your earlier vision and update it if necessary. Then work back and identify what needs to be done and achieved on a month-by-month basis. Keep the plan for year 2 at a high level, but plan the first three months in detail.

Once you have your plan, identify barriers or potential problems that could get in your way. What could go wrong, what could cause this to happen and what can you do to prevent it? Build these actions into the plan.

Finally, you should be as specific as possible about how you will know if you are succeeding. Set key performance indicators that you can monitor on a monthly basis that will let you and your boss know if you are on track. Make sure that at least one indicator tracks the financial benefits of your projects. Be clear about the business benefits that your projects are delivering, as this will help you to justify future investment in you and your team. Businesses spend money to get a return, so the project manager who cannot demonstrate the business benefits of what they are doing is the one who will feel the pinch first when times.

6

TEAM-BUILDING SKILLS FOR PROJECT MANAGERS

Project management is too often seen in terms of 'hard', technical skills and people are trained accordingly. However, increasingly businesses are realizing that it is people skills that are key to the success of projects– it is people who make projects successful rather than systems and processes. Whether you manage projects on a regular basis or only once or twice a year, the skills learned in project management are applicable to many managerial and leadership positions. Understanding client needs and meeting their expectations in a timely manner are universal requirements.

To be a great project manager, you must have an extensive set of skills—from planning and delegation to communication and motivation. Because the skill set is so wide, it's tempting to build skills in the areas of management that you're already comfortable with. However, for your long-term success, it's wise to analyse your skills in all areas of management—and then to challenge yourself to improve in each of these areas.

Building team is a major duty of a project manager. Teams are key tool for organizing work. Teams have the potential to immediately amass, organize, relocate, and disperse. But, teams are an effective tool of employee motivation. It is essential to consider the fact that teams develop and get mature over a period of time. Team development creates a captivating atmosphere by encouraging co-operation, teamwork, interdependence and by building trust among team members.

There are some tasks which can't be done alone. Individuals need to come together, discuss things among themselves and work together towards the realization of a common goal. The individuals forming a team should ideally think more or less on the same lines and should have similar interests and objective. People with absolutely different tastes can't form a team. Their goals have to be the same. Every team is formed to achieve a predefined goal and it is the responsibility of each and every member to contribute his level best and accomplish the assigned task within the stipulated time frame. The team members must complement each other and come to each other's help whenever required. Individual performances do not matter much in a team and every individual should strive hard and work in unison.

The team members don't start performing from the very beginning, they need time. It is not always that all the members would perform equally. Some of them might not get along well with their team mates or have other issues with each other. Individuals sometimes find it difficult to adjust with each other and as a result their performance suffers. Any individual fails to perform; the complete team is at loss. Team management activities ensure that all the team members work together on a common platform for a common goal.

Team management refers to the various activities which bind a team together by bringing the team members closer to achieve the set targets. For the team members, their team must be their priority and everything else should take a back seat. They should be very focused on their goals.

STAGES OF TEAM DEVELOPMENT

A team is a group of individuals, all working together for a common purpose. The individuals comprizing a team ideally should have common goals, common objectives and more or less think on the same lines. Individuals who are not compatible with each other can never form a team. They should have similar if not the same interests, thought processes, attitude, perception and likings.

The four stages of team development are:

Stage 1: Forming

During this stage, group members may be anxious and adopt wait-and-see attitude. They will be formal towards each other. There would be no clear idea of goals or expectations. Besides, they may not be sure why they are there.

This is the stage where the team needs to write its own charter or mission statement as well as clarify goals. The most important thing here is that goals must have a personal buy-in.

By doing this the team will be able to establish boundaries as well as determine what is expected. Team members will get to know each other doing non-conflict laden task. This builds the commitment towards one larger goal.

Thus, during the forming stage, the team members are in process of knowing each other and getting at ease with them.

Stage 2: Storming

During this stage, team members are eager to get going. Conflict can arise as people tend to bring different ideas of how to accomplish goals. At this time, they notice differences rather than similarities. This leads to some members dropping out mentally or physically.

At this stage, communication is important. Tensions will increase. So recognizing and publicly acknowledging accomplishments also become important. It becomes important to participate in meetings and diversity needs to be valued.

Thus, during the storming stage, the team members begin showing their actual styles. They start getting impatient. They try to probe into each other's area, leading to irritation and frustration. Control becomes the key concern during this stage.

Stage 3: Norming

This stage is when people begin to recognize ways in which they are alike. They realise that they are in this together. Hence, they tend to get more social and may forget their focus in favour of having a good time. This is the time to help with training if applicable. It becomes important to encourage them in order to feel comfortable with each other and with systems. Also, the group needs to stay focused on goal.

Thus, during the norming stage, there is conflict resolution. There is greater involvement of team members. There is a greater "we" feeling rather than "I" feeling.

Stage 4: Performing

This stage is when team members are trained, competent, as well as able to do their own problem-solving. At this time, ways need to be looked at in order to challenge them as well as develop them. The team is mature now. The members understand their roles and responsibilities. They would require more input in processes. The members would be self-motivated as well as self-trained. Thus, their efforts need to be recognized. Growth has to be encouraged. This is done by giving new challenges to the team.

Thus, teams at the stage of performing are self-controlling, practical, loyal as well as productive. Focus is there on both performance as well as production.

Forming an Effective Team

This is the general approach to forming a successful work team. But not all will take the same steps. Success is usually hinged on taking all of the steps just discussed. We have a tendency to want to surround ourselves with people who are just like us. In case you get to choose a team, instead of organizing a pre-formed team, then you'll look for a team of people with a variety of strengths. In case of a team that is already in place, organizing can be more subtle. Like, all the workgroups can be called together in order to discuss what goals you want to accomplish and how everybody can help.

You will also find that imposing goals on people doesn't work nearly as well as having them tell you as to what goals they will strive for. But setting goals is not easy work. Too often they end up in being too unrealistic, too vague, impossible to measure, or just stretching into eternity without any deadline.

LEADING THE TEAM

Leadership is an interesting subject because there are so many thoughts on what makes a good leader and so many differing attributes and styles of leadership.

Without effective leadership, a project's chance of success is severely reduced. You can learn all the tools and techniques for effective project management, but if you do not have the ability to bring people with you team will be wasted. To date, books have focused upon the project leader'.

The fundamental difference between a manager and a leader is that if you have all the 'technical' skills and abilities to run a project and understand the complexities of project management as a discipline, you are probably a very good project manager, but there is something missing -a certain x factor that gives some project managers an edge. That is leadership. This difficult-to-define quality basically means an ability to bring people on a 'journey' and get the best out of them, rather than just 'use' human resources. It is leadership that affects the other axis in the matrix below—team effectiveness.

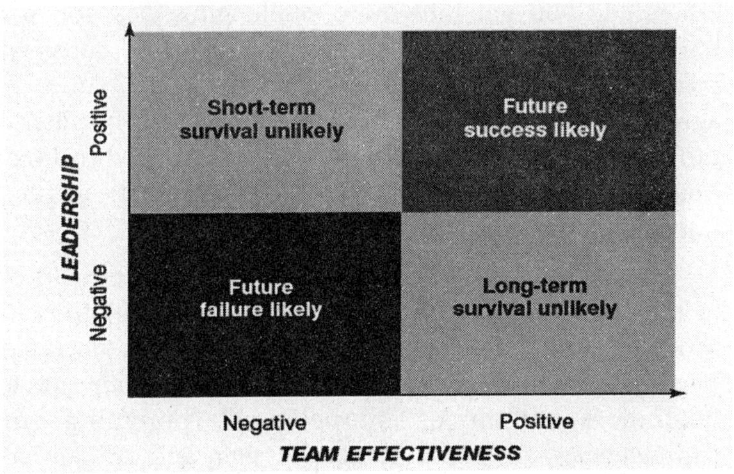

Figure 1

Positive' leadership, as expressed in the matrix, is appropriate to the project situation, while 'negative' leadership is inappropriate to the situation. Leadership is a multifaceted and dynamic skill. It need:

- the right thinking
- the right skills
- the right commitment.

Right Thinking

Self-perception

The starting point for managing an effective project is to manage yourself. Unfortunately, all too often they have not been so diligent with their own personal development planning. If you are a newly promoted manager or have just been made a project manager, make sure you spend some time thinking about how you see yourself in the new role and how you wish to be seen by others. As you get into more challenging jobs you may have to adjust your thinking. Thinking differently will include not only how to deliver projects on time, to the agreed quality and within budget, but also such things as motivating team members and raising standards. Managing time, quality and budget is the starting point, but leadership requires more.

Conducting a self-assessment against four dimensions is a useful starting point: knowledge, competencies, attitudes and behaviours. Do you have the necessary knowledge about changes in the industry, your top ten customers and major competitors? Analyzing your competencies, are you a process thinker, and are you able to conduct analyses to understand why things happen (or could happen), review project management processes and put into place plans that will deliver benefits on time and within budget? Do you have the right attitude in terms of being positive, and in your behaviours do you actively support others in the project management process and have the determination to overcome obstacles?

Before taking action, take time to discuss your thoughts with your boss or your coach. Perhaps summarise your thoughts in the form of a SWOT (strengths, weaknesses, opportunities and threats), before putting a plan together. However, do not be overambitious and try to develop yourself too quickly—becoming an effective project leader takes time.

All roles are different by nature, but the jump from one grade to the next is probably the most pronounced when you first step into management. This is the same for any project manager, especially as most projects involve cross-functional teams and many of the team members will not even report to you. You need to start thinking as a project management professional. While this is likely to be the most enjoyable job you will ever do, it is not something you do for the fun of it—you've got to make money for yourself and your organization. You will also need to be more aware of the whole organization and be proactive in terms of anticipating change. How much time do you spend thinking about the future—is it really enough? One of the key attributes of the Good manager is that they will spend more time looking up and around them at what is happening in other functions or businesses.

Emphasise Balance

The 'three circles', or action centred leadership model developed by John Adair is relevant here. This simple model may not be the latest in management thinking, but good tools always stand the test of time.

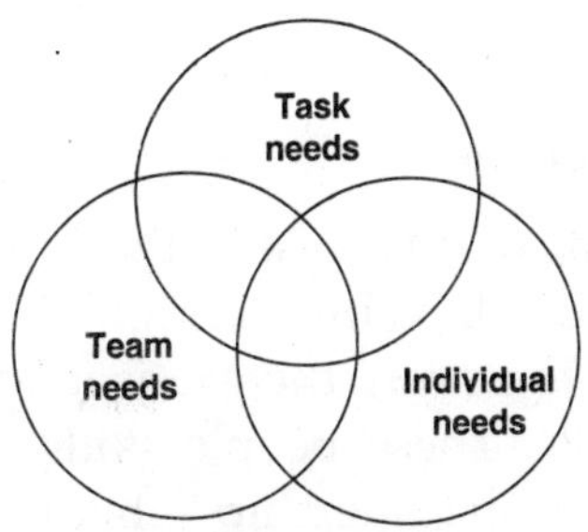

Figure 2

Adair's research suggested that effective leaders (or in case 'project managers') can switch their attention and focus between the three elements of the model: the needs of the team, the task and the individual. Because all are interdependent, the leader must watch all three. Therefore, the real skill or attribute that an effective project manager should develop is the ability to know *when* to focus on the team, the task or the individual. Applying this model to project management helps a Good manager to understand where their emphasis should be at certain times or phases of a project:

- *Task needs.* These are the objectives of the project (i.e. the needs of the business). They will be met by setting clear goals and objectives, creating the right project structure and managing the project through meetings and reports.
- *Team needs.* These are things like effective meetings, support for stakeholders, sharing work, and communication within the team and with other project teams.
- *Individual needs.* These will of course vary from person to person, but the effective project leader will understand how the needs of individuals in the team and the emotional needs of stakeholders should be met.

Right Skills

Technical Versus People

In a project context this means the effective creation of objectives, good planning, effective management of meetings, etc. However, the project leader also needs good people skills. These people skills will inevitably be linked to a 'style' of leadership—this is *how* you interact with others. So, understanding your style of leadership is as important as understanding, say, critical path analysis or Gantt charts.

Leadership Style

These may be your first tentative steps into management or you may be an experienced manager, but in either case take time to reflect on what leadership style may be appropriate for your role as project manager. One way of thinking about this is to consider the extent to which you involve others in events and key decisions. Project leadership is effectively a continuum from command to consensus, as shown below.

COMMAND
Autocratic, no one else involved

↓

QUESTION
1-on-1 fact gathering

↓

CONSULT
1-on-1 opinion seeking

↓

COLLABORATE
Group meeting

↓

CONSENSUS
Group decision

One extreme is to be dictatorial and adopt a 'command and control' style, where you make the decisions in isolation without involving or consulting others. For example, you may decide what the project tasks are and simply tell people to get on with carrying them out. At the other extreme you allow the group to decide the relevant objectives to achieve through a consensus-driven approach.

These are the two extremes of the leadership continuum and there are of course stages between the two. You may choose to ask questions of key managers in order to confirm facts, such as questioning set objectives, or you may consult them individually or as a group and ask their opinion—but then still make the decisions yourself.

So is there a preferred style for the project manager? The reality is that there is no one right or wrong answer and that your choice will vary depending on the situation. Good project managers assess each situation quickly and are then flexible enough to adapt their style based on three criteria—time, commitment and quality, as given below:

1. Involving others increases both the *time* delay in the decision and the number of people and time involved in the decisionmaking process. The extreme is 'analysis-paralysis' where projects have difficulty getting off the ground due to the perceived need to consult everyone involved at the very beginning. In addition, when quick decisions need to be made in order to react promptly to events, bringing others into the decisionmaking process can be counter-productive.
2. The second criteria is *commitment.* So long as the team respects their project manager, and the more involved people feel, the more likely they are to commit to decisions and actively support the implementation of the project and activities.
3. The third dimension is *quality.* There is no point making decisions in isolation if you lack the facts or experience—you will simply be risking the failure of the project and exposing your reputation as a project manager and an effective decision-maker.

Reflect on your style of leadership using the involvement model. What is your preferred style? When would a consensus style be more appropriate and when would a command style be more effective? While everyone has a preferred style, Good project managers are comfortable operating at all points on the continuum, but to do this they will have developed appropriate skills. Some of these skills are given below:

– *Command.* Ability to analyse the situation, solve problems alone, make decisions, proactively think ahead and manage risks, and the willingness and ability to tell others what to do.

– *Question.* Ability to ask open and closed questions and, most importantly, to listen to the answers without interrupting, so that you have sufficient facts to make the decision.

– *Consult.* Willingness and ability to listen hard to what others are telling you, noticing subtler signals such as feelings and opinions, and the ability to seek proposals from others.

– *Collaborate.* Ability to manage meetings effectively with clear objectives, agenda and logistics, as well as a willingness to challenge the group, discuss ways forward and manage conflict where there are differences of opinion.

– *Consensus.* Ability to set group boundaries, build consensus in a team and gain commitment to outputs, while remembering that not everyone needs to agree with the decision of the group, but that they do need to commit to it.

Coaching

While not part of the formal leadership model above, coaching should also play a role in developing yourself as well as members of your team. It is said that if you want to master a particular discipline then teach it. Good managers develop excellent coaching skills—helping individuals develop core skills or resolve barriers.

Right Commitment

Whether people across the business report to you or are simply contributors to your project activities, think carefully about how you will keep them motivated. First, focus on the behaviour you are looking for. It may be that you want people to get involved in the planning of a project or the delivery of a specific task. Whatever it is, people's behaviour will be determined by what comes before they need to do the task, called antecedents, and what comes afterwards, known as consequences:

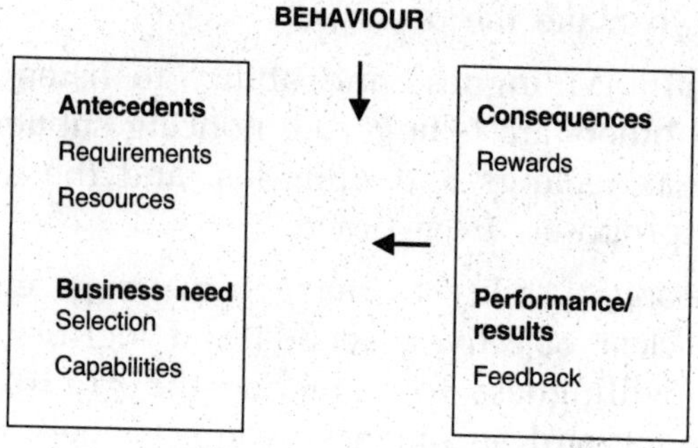

— *Antecedents.* Once you are sure you have chosen the right people for the task, set them up for success by making it clear what is expected of them and what the outcomes should look like. Targets should be stretching but should not over-stretch individuals, as this can be demotivating. Create clear and understandable objectives and tasks. These should reflect the business need at the high level but they should also reflect the experience and skills of project members at a lower level too. Finally, think about the resources individuals will need to be effective. These may include time, facilities, materials, equipment, data and budget.

- *Consequences.* Look closely at each task and assess the natural consequences for each person. This can be distilled down into the 'WIIFM factor'. WIIFM stands for What's in it for me?' If they do a great job, what happens to them or what benefits do they receive? These benefits include not only bonuses, etc. but also other elements that help motivate the individual. Avoid situations where there are positive consequences for doing a bad job. For example, if someone fails to implement a new project effectively because they are keen to move on to a different project, find a way of ensuring this does not happen. Conversely, think of ways to use consequences to drive positive behaviour. For example, if someone arrives late for the start of a project meeting, ask them to capture issues on the flip chart or to take the minutes. The most effective way of keeping people motivated is typically through the use of natural rewards, such as allowing them to present to senior managers, seeing a project through to completion or by you simply taking the time to say 'thank you'.

Think about the next project team meeting you will be running and use the model to check that you have set it up for success. What do you need to put in place in terms of antecedents, and what do you need to do to ensure that the consequences of participating are positive ones? For example:

Antecedents	Ensure that the project relates to a current business imperative
	Put together an invitation to attend that includes the background, a set of objectives and an agenda with timing

Invite the right people to get the right skills and ensure they understand the processes you will be using—hold a five-minute converzation with each to clarify expectations

Ensure the room you have is large enough, has plenty of natural light, encourages creativity and has the appropriate layout

Send an email reminder out a few days beforehand asking all participants to make sure the meeting is in their diaries

Think about the risks—what could go wrong—and plan mitigating actions

Behaviour The team discusses and plans the project to the level of detail you have stipulated

'Success' would be a project plan to which the team commits

Consequences Ensure that the relevant stakeholders are aware of the implications of the project, specifically the resources required

Allocate a budget for a team dinner as a way of encouraging future participation and celebrating success

Arrange for someone else to capture the outputs and circulate them to the team within a couple of days

At the end of the meeting thank everyone for their contributions, picking out one or two people for particular praise.

Create the Right Environment

You and your team may be developing highly complex project plans, but without a supportive culture key stakeholders will not 'buy in', and your project will become just another initiative that quietly disappears. Even though you've given the new project the best chance of success by following a professional process and gathering the right data, you still have to take key individuals with you or your project will quickly fall apart.

An environment that is suitable for effective project management depends on the culture you create as the leader of your team and the physical environment that people work in. Both must work together to support the creative generation of ideas and the rigorous implementation of projects—for project management to flourish and be a success, both of these components are necessary.

The organization may have one culture and the team may exhibit another culture. However, there are basic components that tend to result in an environment that will be more conducive to good project management, irrespective of the culture that dominates in your organization. These include:

- *Creative challenge.* Create an environment of challenge and confrontation, but make sure that it is positive. It is easy to knock a contribution, but make sure when you or a member of the team does that you have an alternative or are prepared to search for one.
- *Blame-free.* When trying to scope projects there is always a degree of uncertainty and risk. This means that people will not always get it right, and not all ideas will be good ideas. Where bad ideas are heavily criticised, people quickly stop putting

forward new concepts or ways of improving projects, for fear of being ridiculed.

- *Ethical boundaries.* Make a choice about what you will and will not be prepared to consider. As well as making a statement about your beliefs—what is right and what is wrong—you will also clarify the boundaries for others. In any industry there will be the possibility of cutting corners, flirting with legality and, for example, behaving in a more or less environmentally green manner. Think about the issues that affect you and your industry and make decisions on the limits you will set. These set the tone for how you will manage other people, as well as manage projects.
- *Learning organization.* Work hard to create a culture where people learn from each other and from past projects. There is nothing more demoralising than running a project that fails, only to find that someone else had already made the very same mistake several years earlier. This is a discipline that needs to be built into the culture of the team. A lessons-learned database for projects is not just a technical requirement for an effective project management office but it also helps to build up the people-skills culture necessary for continuous project improvement.

Role of the Project Management Office

Most organizations do not have a project management office (PMO), so a lot of project management activity takes place in the normal course of events—for example, when a salesperson is meeting a customer or when people are chatting over the coffee machine or having a drink after work. In contrast, in larger organizations there is a place for a project management office. Some of the key functions fulfilled by this office are:

- coaching and developing new staff—providing a centre of project excellence within the business;
- facilitating project teams in project planning and problem-solving—providing a source of advice and support;
- facilitating the formal review of the project or portfolio by a project review group (this process is aided significantly by having the right facilities and equipment constantly at hand, and the more advanced organizations will have a dedicated facility for this purpose);
- managing resources across the portfolio;
- ensuring consistency between projects in terms of systems, etc.;
- formulating project strategy and approach;
- scanning all projects;
- sharing project best practice within the business.

In the PMO the project portfolio will always be visible and keep individual projects aware of the bigger picture. Journals and books will provide access to the latest project management thinking, as well as proven techniques. There will also be an online business library—providing electronic reports covering every aspect of project management as a discipline. The standard project management process will be presented in the form of a flowchart, and there will be checklists and templates covering all subsequent projects. Finally, while the facility encourages a systematic approach to project management, there will be an opportunity for innovation and creative thinking. The office will also encourage insights and learning from project successes and failures, receiving and sharing knowledge across the teams.

Depending on the group, you may choose to use a computer with mind-mapping software connected to a projector screen, or you may choose to use Post-it notes stuck to the wall. In either case, make sure that the process of capturing, consolidating and screening the ideas does not get in the way of new thinking.

BUILDING THE TEAM

Employees are the assets of every organization and its success is directly proportional to the hard work every employee puts in. Individuals must work in a little different and smarter way than the others and always feel motivated to give their best. Effort by a single team member goes unnoticed and every team member should contribute equally. Individuals must be aware what his fellow team members are working on and what he is supposed to do.Team work and team building are essential in corporates to make the organization a better place to work.

One does not gain anything out of unnecessary conflicts. You can't afford to fight with your colleague who sits next to you probably for 7-8 hours, five days a week. We are not machines or battery operated devices, we are human beings and we need people to talk to and discuss various things. One cannot implement things on his own, he needs individuals who can work as critics and evaluate the pros and cons of his concepts.

Team building activities bring employees closer and one feels happy to go to work daily. Individuals start enjoying their work and feel fresh the entire day. Please go through two situations carefully:

– *Situation 1.* Chandran worked with a leading organization and handled a team of five skilled team members. Chandran made sure that he interacted with his team members almost daily. He even enquired about their family members and was always available to them. The team members had the liberty to come up with their issues on an open forum or write to him freely. No wonders his team members always appreciated their team leader and looked up to him. His team members never fought among themselves and willingly helped each other.

– *Situation* 2. Somayya on the other hand also had four individuals directly reporting to him. He always maintained a distance from them and never missed an opportunity to criticise or make fun of his team members. No employee was allowed to enter Somayya's cabin without prior appointment. His team members hated their office like anything and preferred working from home just to avoid Samuel. No body was ready to help each other and everyone worked individually. Their team could never achieve their targets within the stipulated time and there was lots of negativity in their team.

Chandran did nothing great. He just reassured his team members that he is always there for them and they can fall back on him anytime. Somayya never encouraged any team building activity and thus his team always suffered.

Team Building activities improve the relations and strengthen the bond among the employees. Every one strives hard to achieve a common goal.

Please refer to Chandran's example once again. His team members had the liberty to write to him anytime or freely discuss issues with him. There was never a misunderstanding among the team members as everyone knew what the other person was upto.

Team Building activities also reduce the chances of confusions, misunderstandings and in a way making the communication effective. Individual is very clear about his goals and objectives and what exactly is expected from him.

Team Building exercises also increase the trust factor among the employees. If you are sitting next to a driver, whom you don't trust, you will always feel uncomfortable and will never be able to enjoy the ride. If you don't trust your teacher, you can never learn anything from him. You need to trust people. Don't always assume that your fellow employee will speak ill about you in front of your superiors. Trust him, you will feel relaxed.

The productivity increases when individuals work as a team. They tend to divide work among themselves and hence the objectives are achieved at a much faster pace. People take less leaves and concentrate more on their work and eventually the organization benefits.

Individuals feel more positive and confident at work. Stress disappears and it reflects on their work. Chances of mistakes reduce and people stop cribbing and blaming others. There is positivity all around. Allow team members to express themselves freely.

Being a "Hitler" at work will never give you extra points, instead you will find yourself in the bad books of other employees. No one will come to you, when you actually need them. People will be hesitant to support you and you can't perform with enemies all around. Gone are the days when the word "boss" meant a terror to the employees. Now a days the team leader is also a part of a single team, just with some additional responsibilities. Learn to respect your colleagues.

What makes a great team?

So you have a great leadership style that is flexible enough to cope with different project stages and situations, and you have a number of highly motivated and skilled people to work with, but that does not necessarily make them a great team. So what do successful project management teams do that differentiates them from average performers? Read through the following checklist and reflect on what you need to do as leader of the team in order to ensure success.

- The team will have great clarity in its goals and have a real sense of purpose. Good teams will have such clarity of vision that they will know how they want to be remembered long after they have been disbanded. The basic differentiator between a 'group' and a 'team' is a common and enthusiastically agreed goal.
- The team will have a strong and enthusiastic leader. This leader provides direction, is supportive of team members and is willing to shoulder responsibility when things do not go according to plan. They are often not the expert or specialist, but they understand how to bring experts together and get them to perform effectively as a unit.
- Good teams also accept that things will change and can act flexibly in order to bring things back on track. They are willing to reappraise situations quickly but calmly explore creative options for dealing with possible changes and move on.
- They will have shared values and a common set of operating principles. While teams comprise people with a variety of skills and experiences, they need to be unified by common beliefs. Shared values will often provide the team with enormous energy and commitment.
- Ideally, the shared values then extend into a general respect and liking for each other where members of the team trust each other and genuinely have fun working together. The Armed Forces will always ensure that their teams spend

time gaining shared experiences in a safe environment before they are asked to put their lives on the line.

- There will be issues to deal with, but the Good teams will manage these quickly and sensitively before they become crises. To do this they need to have open and honest communication and work in a blame-free environment.
- Finally, the team will be balanced in terms of the skills and capabilities of team members and in terms of the roles they each fulfil. The team will have people capable of creative challenge, but it also needs people willing to get their heads down in order to put the work in and deliver the results. You may want to allocate them roles reflecting different ways of thinking, as illustrated by Edward de Bono's 'six hats'.
  - *White Hat*—Focus on evidence and the facts
  - *Red Hat*—Focus on emotion and gut feel
  - *Yellow Hat*—Focus on the positive – why it will work
  - *Green Hat*—Focus on lateral thinking and brainstorming
  - *Black Hat*—Focus on the negative – devil's advocate
  - *Blue Hat*—Focus on evaluation – pros and cons

  You may not wish to allocate these roles, but reflecting on which of your team members operate naturally wearing one of these hats will help you to make the most of your people and plug potential gaps.

Frequently project teams operate as a 'virtual team', working across functions and geographic boundaries. In these cases the principles of good teams become even more important, since the influence of the leader is dissipated either by hierarchical control or geographic distance.

DEVELOPING THE SKILLS

As well as developing the skills of individual members of your team, you need to build them into a strong and effective team.

Next, assess where you think the team is now in terms of its stage of development. This is particularly important for those working in the area of project management, as teams are often part-time—coming together for events such as project team meetings or the implementation of an initiative. Each team will go through various stages of development, and your role as the leader will be to recognize where they are and to take action to move them to a state where they are their most productive.

Having goals or a clear purpose is important to each of us. In fact, people who set goals are always more successful than the others. For leaders who are serious about setting goals, some things are to be kept in mind. These goals need to be Specific, Measurable, Attainable, Realistic, and with Timelines.

Besides, for any organization, goals should also be expressed positively. And for a team, goals need to be personalised for each member of the team. All these goals should be put in writing, where you as well as the team can see them often. Once you sit down with your team and set some goals, it can be very useful to develop some kind of action plan for accomplishing that goal.

Informality as well as Participation

In order to build an effective team, the climate has to be informal, comfortable, as well as relaxed. There should be no tension or any signs of boredom. Teams enjoy getting together, they interact easily. There should be lots of good-natured kidding and laughter. Have seating arrangements in order to facilitate this. A circle is the best seating arrangement usually, while a typical classroom arrangement is the worst.

Listening

A highly efficient team has team members who use effective listening techniques. These include questioning, paraphrasing, as well as summarising in order to get out ideas. Listening is the most effective factor that distinguishes effective teams from ineffective teams.

The ability to really listen is a highly important skill. Each team member has to have it. Listening lets you understand what the other person is saying. Besides, it shows the other person that you're interested in what he/she has to say. But all of us experience common listening problems.

We tend to let our attention wander. Our mind drifts away. We start thinking about the time, or other tasks at hand. This way we lose our concentration.

We miss the real point of what is being said. We may end up focusing on the personality of the speaker. Else we may let our judgement of the person based on past experiences come in the way. Or, we may be trying hard to look for hidden messages and lose out on the crux of the conversation.

Our emotions interfere with our judgment. This takes away our focus from what is being said. Our judgement of the person interferes with our understanding of what is being said.

We tend to interrupt and step on the statements of others. This way we don't listen to what is being said. Besides, there is a tendency to think ahead to what we want to say next and miss out on what's being said right now. It is important to use the steps of active listening in order to be a good listener.

ROLE OF MOTIVATION AND ATTITUDE IN TEAM

A team is formed when individuals with a similar interest come together to realise a common dream. The team members must think of their team first and all other personal interests should come later. Every individual must contribute equally as per his capability to achieve the predefined targets successfully within the desired time frame.

Motivation and attitude go hand in hand in increasing the output of any team.

You need a match stick for fire, you need ink for a pen to write, and similarly an individual needs motivation to perform. Every individual has some latent talent and needs a push for the talent to come out. Without motivation, the team members feel reluctant to work and also tend to spread negativity around. Human beings are hungry for praise and appreciation. It is the prime duty of the team leader to appreciate his team members whenever they have done something great. This way they feel happy and motivated to perform even better the next time.

Set a deadline for the submission of work. All the employees submitting the work within the stipulated time frame must be appreciated in public. Circulate a mail among all the employees appreciating your team member's efficiency. Any person coming out with a brilliant idea should be suitably rewarded. It is not always you give cash to motivate your employees, but even small tokens of appreciation can make a difference. Reward your team member with anything he likes. Appreciating one member does not mean you will neglect or criticise the other members of the team who could not perform up to the mark this time. It is the duty of the team leader to motivate them so that they perform well the next time. Ask them to "BUCK UP".

A single member's performance can hardly make a difference to the team's performance; every member has to contribute equally for the maximum output. Celebrate your team's success inviting all your team members. Take them out for a lunch to a nearby restaurant. They will feel happy and also come closer to each other this way. Give a pat on their back to appreciate their hard work.

Titles such as "Best Employee of the month" and "Best Team Member" also go a long way in motivating the team members. The names of the best performers must be displayed on the notice boards for everyone to see.

Incentives and perks also motivate the employees to a large extent. If any team member does something outstanding do not forget to appreciate him on an open forum and also ask the other members to reach to his level as well.

Avoid making fun of your colleagues. It is considered highly unprofessional. Don't spread negativity around. Don't depend on blame games or spread unnecessary rumours about your team members.

Motivation alone can't create wonders; it needs to be coupled with positive attitude of the team members to ensure high performance of the team. Adopt a positive attitude at work. Do not always find faults in others. Listen to your team members as well. Don't assume things or draw conclusions on your own. Be a little more flexible and adjusting to avoid conflicts at work place. Sit and discuss issues with your team members to reach to an alternative. Results can't be achieved unless and until you believe in yourself. The will power to do something is important. One should have the urge to perform.

Always try to look at life from a larger perspective. Things can not always be the way you like, its better to accept things as it is sometimes. Remember after heavy rains, there is always a clear sky. Problems might crop up anytime, but it is always better to grin and move on. Do not overreact on petty things.

Don't be too adamant or rigid, instead be a little forgiving. It is absolutely okay if you take the initiative and say "Sorry". This magical word goes a long way in reducing conflicts to a large extent. Don't unnecessary create tensions for others and yourself as well.

Don't be disheartened if some one comes to you and corrects you for your mistakes; do take it in a positive and healthy way. Do not step in the office with a mind clouded with negative thoughts. Everything seems wrong to you and you unnecessarily fight with people around.

Team members must adopt a positive attitude to avoid tensions and misunderstandings at work place. Positive attitude with a little motivation can actually create wonders for the team.

7

CHALLENGES OF PROJECT MANAGERS

Today, project management has become a mainstream skill for all managers, irrespective of sector, discipline or management level. There are two separate paths down which managers new to project management could go.The first option is that of a full-time, 'professional' project manager. If that is your chosen route and you wish to make project and programme management your chosen area of expertise, then you should look towards getting some sort of accreditation through some bodies. Find out what is appropriate for you and take steps to move towards becoming a professional full-time project manager. The second path is to develop your project management skill or expertise, without it becoming your central job or role. Here, you develop your project management expertise within the context of your current job area. For example, it could be becoming more experienced in project management within marketing or sales or in customer services. Those job areas will probably guide your promotion and job path, but well-developed skills in project management will be a distinguishing factor that will help you stand out amongst your peers. It is no less professional than option one, but the career development path differs greatly in terms of emphasis and qualifications.

PERFORMANCE INDICATORS

Whether they opt for full-time project management or use project management skills as part of their job, Good managers should know what is important and what is not. They focus on the Key Performance Indicators (KPIs) that have the greatest impact upon the business. They regularly take time to reflect on the past in order to learn from what went wrong or what could be improved, and they think ahead to the future so that concerns can be resolved before they become crises. By always delivering beyond expectations, they stand out from the pack and will be automatic considerations for promotion at the appropriate time. This is, of course, true for all disciplines and areas of expertise, but getting a reputation for delivering results, on time and within budget, is critical for project leaders.

Review Past Performance

In terms of driving performance in the business and getting to the top in your chosen area of project management, experience tells us that an understanding of past performance is a very good starting point. As a good project manager you should review, at a macro level how your projects and the company as a whole have performed over the last strategic period—say two to three years. What is the trend and what are the specific problems holding back projects or performance? Ask yourself how you are going to gather that information and how others will be able to learn from it.

Current Priorities

Having seen what has happened in the past, it may be worth looking at current initiatives and whether the so-called 'performance gap' will be closed. Those involved in managing projects and programmes will need to understand the following:

- What programmes are underway to improve project management performance?
- What projects are underway and what is their likelihood of success—i.e. are they on track?
- What mechanisms are in place to deal with any project issues that arise?

Relate these findings to the audit data found previously. Is there a trend? To get to the top within project management within your business, you do need to address the environment in which projects and programmes are delivered, as well as ensuring that the individual projects you are managing are successful.

Future Intentions and Actions

By taking a view wider than that of simply improving individual projects—that is, engineering the project environment in which your projects operate—you will be taking a longer-term, strategic view of project and programme management. This has benefits out of all proportion to the effort invested in assessing past projects and planning new ways of doing things. It is precisely this approach that marks out strategic thinkers against other competent project managers. Always be thinking about how to improve the way projects are managed—the process—as well as how to deliver the value of an individual project—the content.

At the top of the business, directors are always encouraged to take the longer view and to think in terms of improving processes rather than projects. For the Good project manager, this is always a good tip to follow, if you want to get on in the future.

CHALLENGE YOURSELF

The easiest thing to do is to rest on one's laurels, but in modern business it is a reputation for driving change that is sought after and valued. Look for ways to introduce challenge to you and your team on a regular basis, aiming to bring in ideas, tools and techniques from recognized leaders in the area of project and programme management.

When possible, setup systems or processes to gather and glean information from different groups. Consider groups that may not think like you and may have a different 'take' on how your projects should be managed or approached. These could include:

- *Other departments and teams within your company.* In a large organization there may be other teams managing projects very successfully, using systems, techniques and processes unknown to you. Creating an internal 'community of practice' (CoP) where you can share ideas (good, bad or indifferent) is a great way to challenge yourself and your own thinking.
- *Customers.* Have you ever thought about how customers manage their projects? Maybe a customer or client out there is an expert in a certain field or area of project management. You may only see them as a purchaser of your products or services but there may be more to the relationship than meets the eye. Move away from this one-dimensional view of your customer and look at them as a project partner (when appropriate)—it may pay dividends. For example, Patrick recalls a large multinational bank's PMO (project management office). They were the guardians of the bank's project management process and organized training events as well as the publishing

of the project management guide for the bank. They were very happy for any client or supplier of theirs to understand and/or adopt their systems and processes, since they viewed this as a means of working more closely with a client.

- *Competitors.* What are your competitors doing now that could be copied? How are you going to get that information? Many people forget that when new hires start work in your business they are a rich source of information. However, they are often only quizzed on their content expertise (*what* they know) and not on past employers' systems and processes (*how* they did things). Don't be precious about using other people's approaches to managing projects. Customize, beg, borrow and rework—all are valid tactics when trying to improve the management of your projects and programmes.
- *Supply chain.* Just as customers may have a good way of doing things, your suppliers may have too. In fact many businesses actively seek to align core business processes to improve the supply of goods and services to the marketplace, and aligning your project management process to that of your suppliers is an ideal way of getting synergies and benefits. With online project reporting tools and projects that include many supplier tasks and inputs, projects can be speeded up and risks greatly reduced if there is a 'symbiotic' relationship or association between suppliers and the supplied.
- *Industry experts.* What are the experts recommending for your business sector? What breakthrough tools and techniques have they developed? Have you linked up with special interest groups (SIGs) within project management bodies. Here you are looking for content

knowledge (what?) as well as project management process knowledge (how?).

UPDATE YOUR KNOWLEDGE

As well as working with other groups inside and outside the business, think carefully about what additional sources of knowledge and insight you want to receive and how often. There is a wealth of information available from a variety of sources, so you need to be selective, as the time you have available for reading is limited and the quality can be variable. Keeping up to date should not be a chore or burdensome, so being selective and specific is key. Too much searching and too much 'data' (as opposed to 'knowledge') can rapidly become distracting and diverting.

There are numerous places to look for information on the latest in project and programme management. Select a few tried and trusted sources and try to be specific in terms of the information you are searching for. Most online websites have a mechanism by which you can ask for new postings or information to be emailed to you at a certain frequency—monthly, weekly or even daily. Look for the following sources:

- *Journals or trade magazines.* There are some standard publications in the area of project management that will often have information on latest thinking or tools and techniques. But also look for trade journals in your area of business or sector and see if they have sections on project management too.
- *Track-recommendation:* try to get your company to subscribe to one journal of greatest relevance for one year and then review its value. Make sure you circulate it within the company once you have read it.

- *Conferences.* These provide a useful source of usually new information. They are also good places to network. However they can be very time consuming and expensive. Good recommendation: it pays to get the conference agenda in advance and cherry-pick the sessions that are of the most interest and relevance to you. Aim to identify those people who are relevant to your issues and plan to follow up with them afterwards.
- *Communities of practice (CoPs).* These are online discussion forums between like-minded people within specific areas of the project management 'community'. Good recommendation: these can be extremely useful or a complete waste of time, so give them a go and see what value you get. Many CoPs in project management are focused around certain software platforms or specific methodologies, so beware of being involved in something too specific too early on, as their relevance to you might be limited. You may also want to consider forming your own forum, but remember that you will need to put in the necessary time and effort to get it off the ground.
- *Web.* This provides freely available information from many sources, but it is usually unstructured and potentially distracting as you wade through the mountains of unrelated material. Good recommendation: treat searching the internet as a serious activity and not as surfing. Be specific with your searches and set yourself specific timescales to gather information. Once you have found useful sites, bookmark them and become active within the site by asking for information and providing comments or data.
- *Professional bodies.* The more senior you become, the more important and useful these bodies can be to

you and your organization, as they are often a source of free advice and networking. Good recommendation: once you have been in your role for at least a year, sign up for an initial trial period and see what benefits you receive. Gather information from third parties about the rival membership organizations and look at independent sites for recommendations. In the world of project management, the APM and PMI are two very good starting points, but do your own research. There are many smaller groups focusing upon specific project management areas.

– *Personal networks.* Never underestimate personal networks. Many of these individuals are on the intersection between academia and practice and most, if not all, are self-employed. The increasing propensity for experienced individuals to work on their own as contractors in a 'portfolio career' has generated a whole workforce of experienced individuals who are not obviously affiliated to professional bodies, websites or CoPs.

Remember that, whatever your source of information, to maximize the benefits you need to put time aside and make the necessary effort. However, also recognize that you will never have perfect knowledge—particularly in the area of project management, as it is such a wide and expanding area of expertise. Decide what level of information will be good enough and then act on it. In experience the best project managers and directors have their own trusted circle of advisers, virtual or actual, where they go not only for the latest information and techniques but also for advice and for someone to bounce ideas off.

GET PROMOTED

It is difficult to specify what you, as a good project

manager, need to do to get promoted, as conditions will change and the criteria for promotion will vary from company to company. In fact very few people now look at a career within a single company and so promotion may mean moving outside a company. Identify whether your company has a 'talent pool' in terms of a recognized high-potential programme for all managers.

Whatever your area of expertise and chosen profession, take time to reflect on your state of readiness for promotion. Identify the future role you are keen to fulfil; clarify the criteria you will need to satisfy in terms of skills, experience, attitudes and behaviours; and consider how you will visibly demonstrate these attributes to others. Ask yourself the following:

- *Capability.* Do have what it takes in terms of what have achieved and learned so far? How can demonstrate capabilities in terms of managing projects?
- *Credibility.* Can convince others that can and will perform the role well? Can get third-party or client testimonies to attest to skills as a project manager?
- *Desire.* Do want the role and do have sufficient drive and enthusiasm to do a great job? Ask yourself why you want a new role or challenge and then how you would demonstrate this to potential employees—without coming across as desperate.
- *Relationships.* Do have positive working relationships with the right people? For internal promotions this is a key factor. Getting along with people may be more important that certain technical skills and competencies, which can be attained later on. Demonstrating your skill at building relationships is the Holy Grail at interviews—according to the HR director of a major UK utility company.

- *Competitive.* The most appropriate candidate given the internal and external alternatives? Of course you are! Next question.

If you have concerns, then put in place a plan to address them. Timing will be key, so make sure you are well prepared before putting yourself forward for a role.

In terms of increasing your project management responsibility alongside that of your professional role, there is usually a hierarchy within project and portfolio management. In ascending order of complexity and seniority, the roles are often:

- project manager
- programme manager (a programme being multiple related projects)
- project (programme) management office manager
- project sponsor
- project director.

BECOMING A DIRECTOR

Most of them have a separate discipline or expertise in addition to their project management skills and experience—be it new product development, marketing or customer services. In addition, in some organizations the responsibility for managing or overseeing the portfolio of projects at strategic level might be allocated to a specific director, such as the director of marketing, R&D or operations.

Whatever the title, the director in charge of projects or programmes will fulfil various roles in addition to meeting their statutory responsibilities. These include:

- *Linking projects to business strategy.* This is the so-called strategic project management (SPM) function and requires an understanding of the business strategy but also of the current project capabilities of the business.

- *Championing projects.* If project management is a discipline central to the success of the business, then ensuring that projects have specific resources and sufficient budgets in the face of internal competition from other areas will be a key responsibility.
- *Creating a progressive project management environment.* This means ensuring that a culture exists in which projects can be managed professionally and thoroughly. This requires a knowledge of what technology exists to help project managers and what would be appropriate for the business, including the impact of trends in project management (technology) and the impact on the business and projects underway.
- Managing the project management office (PMO). The role here is to get a strategic picture for the board of what projects are underway, the risks involved and the progress to date. Reporting the current projects underway at board level is often a sore point, as unfortunately many boards of directors underestimate the number of projects in progress—some by as much as half.
- Managing project resources. Some organizations devolve project resources to certain departments or disciplines, while some keep them centralised and get departments to bid for the budget and resources in terms of what the projects will deliver. In either scenario, the project director has to track resources against value and results.

In addition to these formal roles, a project director will probably be involved in informally reviewing and auditing project work, as well as mentoring or coaching project managers. These would be useful skills for a new project manager to acquire.

Whatever the style of the project director or the organization of the business, strategic project management is about three interrelated influences, which are different from those at the lower project management level. Whereas at project management level it is about time, cost and performance, at strategic level it is about strategy, resources and results.

Reaching the Top

In project management the 'top' can take many forms. For many people the top lies not within their company as a project director but as an acknowledged expert in an area of project management. They define success as being an expert who is brought in to help companies out when projects are in trouble. Success is being acknowledged as an independent, project troubleshooter.

One reason why people do not associate the role of director of projects with that of being a project 'expert' is because many businesses see project management as an associated *additional* skill which enhances the specific 'trade' skills of managers—such as marketing, operations, finance, etc. So success is achieved by promotion from project manager through programme manager to a position of seniority within a discipline, i.e. marketing. Project management is thus seen as a means to getting promotion within a discipline, not as a profession in itself.

In fact, for an increasing number of people success in project management is synonymous with independence from full-time employment—meaning you don't have to be employed full-time as an 'expert' project manager to be at the top. It is a skill or discipline that will always be in demand; with a good reputation it is possible to build up a 'portfolio career' gaining project management experience in many different areas, either by joining the company or as a contractor. Many people think that if the situation requires it, a good project manager could step back into full-time employment and use their acquired skills to get back on the career path within a company. Indeed, many businesses are looking at this 'flexible career' mechanism as a means of getting good project managers in when required, but allowing them to get varied experience elsewhere if necessary.

No matter what the 'top' looks like to project managers and directors, many people agree that experience and a good track record in project management, with some degree of formal training, is invaluable. It seems to be that getting to the top in project management nowadays allows individuals a greater degree of flexibility and independence than ever before. Whatever your definition of success, you should plan ahead. If you want to be a self-employed project manager, then you must understand the needs of your specific target market and skill yourself accordingly.

❖❖❖

8

HOW TO SUCCESSFULLY MANAGE EXPECTATIONS?

The world of project management is a tough, hands-on environment that requires project managers to leave their cubicles and get into the fray. People who work on projects don't have time for theory or weeks to learn yet another new process to get the job done. Attempting to create successful project teams through the use of squishy-sounding words like these is often derided as the use of soft skills. But the ability to get work done by understanding people is vastly undervalued in the project management world.

New processes and tools, with metrics and quantitative data are preferred by many project managers because they seem to provide actionable data and create the appearance of positive action when implemented. Managers who put these tools into place often only appear to be doing something useful. The last thing the world needs is another process that requires certification—these cult-like saviors of process, with guardians at the gate preventing qualified people from becoming project managers because they don't know the secret password.

Strong skills are rooted in three concepts:

- Constant respect for all individuals, including individual contributors on the team, the customer, the management food chain involved in the project, and yourself, the project manager.
- Successful leadership through the people—customer, management, and team—involved, using whatever tool or process the organization deems appropriate.
- Conceptualised and articulated principals of leadership that are put into action.

The goal for the project team is more than just meeting the schedule, cost, and performance requirements. The larger goal for teams is always to grow the capabilities of each team member, as well as of the overall team, so that the team will continue to function at a high level long after the project manager has gone on to the next assignment. Success of a project means meeting stakeholder expectations for schedule, cost, and scope while maintaining quality, as well as ensuring that the team grows in overall capability and is a more potent force than when you joined the team.

There are seven characteristics in a succesful project management system. They are:

- Transparency
- Accountability
- Communication
- Trust
- Integrity
- Leadership that drives needed change
- Execution results

Virtually all organizations include values of one sort or another in their mission statements, but there also can be a good deal of cynicism present within those organizations about those mission statements.

It is essential that you, as a project manager, develop the philosophical underpinnings of your approach to managing your projects. To blindly jump into leading any group of people without these underpinnings will leave you like a boat at sea without a guide to shore when storms come.There is no magic here. These seven characteristics are what found to be essential.

Each of these seven characteristics is important in any action taken as a project manager. All of them, or your equivalent list, should be planned into any approach for leading a team.

TRANSPARENCY

Transparency can be defined as the project manager's ability to ensure that the team members are told the truth about organizational policies, business climate, and decisions that affect them.

The term transparency is used widely in the business and political world to convey openness and clarity, when just the opposite can be true. This understandably often leaves people quite cynical about transparency, but, for the leader, modeling transparency is the easiest, quickest way to start down the road toward a cohesive and highly functioning team. This is because the leader can start creating transparency the moment the team is first assembled. The other characteristics require more time and effort.

How to quickly create transparency? Just learn what the team cares about and communicate about those things. Team members desperately want information about what matters to them and care little about other information. Deducing what information is important to them can be tricky in an organization of introverted technical people! Often, they just want to know when the breaks will be, what snacks will be offered, and where the restrooms are.

To find out what your team cares about, start by making a list of what you care about. Then, starting with your staff or the key functional managers for the team, ask for input. Also have skip-level one-on-one meetings with individual contributors (workers) below your staff or your direct reports. Do this in a relaxed, open way so that they do not feel pressure.

If you just cannot bring yourself to manage a probing interactive converzation, that's okay. This is not rocket science. People usually want to know about (1) how the business is doing overall, (2) how the local organization is faring in the ongoing corporate competition between sites, and (3) how the project is perceived by key stakeholders. In lieu of any information from the team members about what they want to hear, you can start with these three items and do the following:

- Share the information periodically in an all-hands meeting.
- Be ready between such meetings to answer team member questions.
- Dedicate a section of your staff meeting to those subjects.

How do you address sensitive areas such as potential layoffs or talk about project cancellations or site closures? These are the very subjects people want to know about, so you cannot ignore them. First, quote as fact only statements that have been made public through your organization's HR group. Start all answers with public information releases and then carefully (oh so carefully!) address areas of interest where you are on firm ground.

Learn how to speak about them with truth and empathy—while protecting your organization—in a way that you would want to be communicated with, and you will be fine.

For example, many managers would refuse to address a question about a rumour about site closure. Prabhakar, a project manager with high levels of empathy, got this exact question during an all-hands meeting at his location, far from the corporation's headquarters. Only then did she ask a question of her own, with an earnest look and a small smile: "Does that make sense?" When he smiled slightly and nodded, she maintained eye contact for another instant and then politely asked if there were more questions.

Project and senior leaders routinely express concern about talking too often and/or sharing excessive information with teams. They are worried about the time required and the distraction of too much information and fear that the team might not want to take the time for so much communication. Lest you as a leader listen to those concerns and do nothing about transparency, ponder this. If a leader is not transparent with a team about the things the team cares about, members will spend a lot of time filling in the lack of information with their own worries and anxieties and gossip. As a result, they will work less efficiently, as the following story illustrates.

Neeraj, a Texas-based project controls manager for a large global technology corporation headquartered in Silicon Valley, noticed the trouble his organization had with transparency during a period of reorganization. The organization held all-hands meetings using an Internet call-in system that allowed presentation on myriad personal computers worldwide, with an international call-in number for audio interaction. The calls usually originated from the corporate headquarters in San Jose,

California. The frequency of these all-hands meetings increased greatly during the reorganization, as leaders tried to clearly communicate the process and the details.

The employees at Neeraj's site would gather in a common room for the calls. To minimize background noise, it was traditional to mute telephones at the nonpresenting locations. As the corporate leaders presented information, Neeraj noticed just how non-transparent was the culture within the organization. With the telephone muted, people around the room would openly speculate on what the person speaking really meant in terms of reporting relationships, organizational structure, and similar issues. Occasionally, someone in the room would un-mute the telephone and ask a question, almost always in a seemingly polite nonconfrontational way that reflected none of the feelings expressed when the phone had been muted. Neeraj quickly became aware that the managers in San Jose had little understanding of the real concerns and issues of the local employees. Discussion with peers at other sites revealed much the same feeling.

After the calls, many of the attendees at Neeraj's site, now thoroughly irritated and dismayed, would continue grumbling and rumbling through the halls on the way back to their cubicles. Those who went out to lunch—the calls typically occurred right before lunchtime in Texas—would continue to try to parse out exactly what was going on and what the presenters had really meant. Needless to say, a great deal of productive work time was lost to gossip and speculation. Neeraj's efforts to raise awareness around the issue went nowhere. Senior leaders were not uninterested; they were just under great time and task pressure and essentially did not know how to react to what Neeraj told them. The organization continued to lose a lot of productivity throughout (and after) the almost two months of reorganization.

ACCOUNTABILITY

Accountability can be defined as the project manager's ability to ensure that everyone on the team knows and executes his or her role, feels empowered and supported in that role, knows the roles of the other team members, and acts upon the belief that those roles will be performed.

Accountability is a misunderstood concept. Many managers act as if accountability means getting in the face of those who make mistakes to make sure they get the reaming they deserve so that they will not mess up again. Senior managers often tell project managers, "You are accountable for the project. I'll be coming to you whenever anything goes wrong." That is only half right. Accountability— to be effective—has to extend to everyone on a team. You as project leader are accountable, but so are the team members and senior management. Management has a different role to play, certainly, but it cannot be completely distanced from the project and expect success.

Start the process of accountability early. Accountability is all about defining roles and responsibilities for each person on the team and holding everyone to them. In one of your first converzations with team members, tell them briefly how you are going to hold yourself accountable and what you, in turn, expect of them. A carefully chosen sentence or two is all that is needed.

Call a special staff meeting the first week you take over the project, and have this discussion. Be sure you discuss roles and responsibilities with newly assigned people soon after they join the team. Roger Connors and Tom Smith, cofounders of a leading firm for accountability training, discuss an "accountability conversion" in How Did That Happen: Holding People Accountable for Results the Positive, Principled Way. You must take these actions to create the right culture on your team. If you do not, some sort of team culture will develop, and it may not be the one you want.

Then have a project kickoff meeting to drive your desired culture. Include a brief discussion of your key values as they apply to executing business results within the team. You should plan on spending time teaching people how to provide accountability for themselves and others in a constructive way. There may be some raised voices along the way. That is okay. Once the right culture takes hold, you will have a powerful team. A culture of mutual accountability leads to winning project teams.

COMMUNICATION

Communication is the project manager's ability to ensure that needed information flows quickly and seamlessly to where it can be used with optimal efficiency.

To be effective, you need to get people talking freely and openly about the right information. You do so by asking questions and actively listening. Spend some time putting yourself in their shoes and thinking like they do. Once you understand their needs and concerns, you will become a better project leader.

For efficient communication to occur—in other words, for information to flow from wherever it is to wherever it needs to go—accountability must already be in place, certainly by planning. If team members know each other's roles and what is expected of each person early on, they will also know whom to talk to about different issues. People normally do not know whom to talk to about detailed issues unless this is the focus of someone in project leadership, and it is especially true on a large global project involving hundreds of employees in crash mode, that is, when many new people are being added all at once. If working-level followers cannot figure out whom to talk to about an issue, they will ask their immediate leader, who also may not know the details of other functional teams. In any case, working through a leader in this way wastes time and does not help followers learn how to work together. Your job is to get the team to work together so that needed information flows quickly and accurately. There is no time to waste.

To make all this work, your functional leaders and staff also have to learn to work together as a unit. Nick, a project manager with responsibility for a variety of different functions, taught his staff how to work together on real issues by changing the structure of weekly team meetings from boring recitations of the week's technical progress to action-oriented discussions where participants explored—as a team—the solutions to issues that affected more than one function. The actions that ensued were then captured in SMART format: Specific, Measurable, Attainable, Realistic, and Timely. The assigned actions would be due sometime in the next week. Long-term issues were broken down into week-size chunks. The team began to work together, and Nick brought the project to a timely and successful conclusion.

The larger issue under discussion may take time to resolve, but people need short-term actions to galvanize and focus their efforts. Once your staff implements this approach, the managers in their organizations will begin to model the behaviour within their teams, and you will be on your way to creating the culture you are looking for.

For more reasons than just good communication, you need to have weekly one-on-one meetings with all direct reports. The meetings are not a chance for you to beat them up or to tell them how to do their jobs but rather should be pegged to their agenda—what they want to talk about, factors that affect their ability to do assigned tasks or grow into new roles. The meetings should be geared toward helping them learn how to lead more efficiently and thoughtfully, and you should be a model for the desired behaviors. Ideally, your direct report should talk approximately 80 per cent of the time. If you are talking, you are not listening.

Your role is to ask the right questions and to offer advice and direction only after your followers have exhausted ideas on what actions need to be taken. Ideally, they should also be implementing 80 per cent of the action items that arise during the meeting. You should help only with problems they cannot solve themselves. Be sure that the action items you do take are high priorities on your list of things to do, people to see, and places to go. That demonstrates, through action, that their needs matter.

TRUST

Trust is the project manager's ability to promote one agenda for all team members—the team's overall goal—and to create a culture in which team members believe they are being told the truth in all interactions.

Trust within the team is the ultimate goal for a project manager— actually, for any leader. Trust comes after the leader has been implementing the preceding characteristics at least reasonably well. The team will grant trust as it buys into the overall plan.

Great things occur on teams when there is trust. This is why sports teams, as well as business teams, can improve dramatically when a change in management approach occurs, as opposed to simply introducing new tools and processes. An example of this in the sports world is what Mike Krzyzewski was able to accomplish with the U.S. Olympic basketball team at the Beijing Olympics in 2008 after previous coaches and U.S. national teams had underachieved for many years. In The Gold

Standard, about the 2008 Olympic experience, Krzyzewski relates his comments at the first team meeting. He said, "Two concepts are fundamental to a team dynamic: communication and trust".

INTEGRITY

Integrity is the project manager's ability to show team members that a consistent set of values or beliefs is being used appropriately to make the correct difficult decisions; also, his or her ability to integrate the efforts of all involved on the project toward the common goal.

If a team follows your leadership, it will do so largely because of two aspects of your integrity: (1) the set of values that encapsulates what you stand for and how you make decisions, and (2) your ability to integrate the individuals on the team into a whole to help them reach their goals by achieving the team's common goal.

Establish your own set of business values based on your personal integrity. You don't have to advertise your beliefs, because actions speak louder than words. In fact, it will be counterproductive if you do. Do tell your teams what your beliefs are, but then model those values in your actions and decisions. Your teams will follow you consistently, and this will generate better business results.

You will fail if you try to implement the other characteristics without having thought out your own personal sense of integrity and without understanding that your job is the integration of individuals into a team. This is often why the introduction of new project management processes and tools fail to provide the desired results.

LEADERSHIP THAT DRIVES NEEDED CHANGE

It is the project manager's ability to plan and execute the

appropriate culture change within the team to drive the actions required for the desired business results.

Good things in life do not happen without some sort of plan, certainly not on complex endeavours like a modern knowledge worker project. To make all these abstract concepts work on your team, you must plan how you are going to make it happen. That is where leadership when making culture changes comes in.

First, evaluate how much culture change is actually required to be successful. This is not a one-sise-fits-all process; in fact, the greatest value in this approach comes from its flexibility. If you are taking over an existing team, ask these questions:

- Does the team have an overall team goal?
- What are the structure and agenda of staff/team meetings?
- Are all-hands meetings occurring? If so, what are the agenda and periodicity?
- How does important information move around?
- How does important information get to the project manager for monthly operations reviews with management? How effectively is that information communicated to management? What does management do with the information?
- What is the approach around schedule and cost control and around metrics, headcount, and risk management? Who owns the updating of this information?

Decide which of these areas you want to change first, and integrate that change into an approach that incorporates the previous five characteristics.

EXECUTION RESULTS

Its is the project manager's ability to blend the other six

characteristics to produce the desired business execution results.

The six characteristics previously discussed, if planned and executed properly, will lead to the execution results your organization desperately craves. Knowledge worker teams do not want to hear these squishy words, so don't talk much about the words but, rather, use them as the basis for how work will get done.

EXPECTATIONS MANAGEMENT

One of the old warhorses in project management is the triple constraints triangle (Figure 1), where the three constraints shown are time, cost, and performance (performance is often also called requirements or scope). Altering any of these three constraints requires that they be traded off against at least one of the others.

Figure 1: Traditional Triple Constraints Triangle

All three cannot be improved simultaneously. For example, if you want to improve a schedule's finish date, you have to allow higher cost and/or lower performance. As is often done, quality has been added inside the triangle to show that quality is always required and cannot be traded off. Most project managers deal quite well with linear tradeoffs of these three technical constraints.

Much complexity occurs when the expectations of your customer, management, and team are added on top of the schedule, cost, and performance technical constraints. Many project managers do not approach the problem this way, continuing to try to trade off the technical constraints, while either ignoring or caving in to the inputs from stakeholders. The inability to balance the expectations of the three stakeholder groups causes more project managers to fail than do schedule, cost, and performance issues.

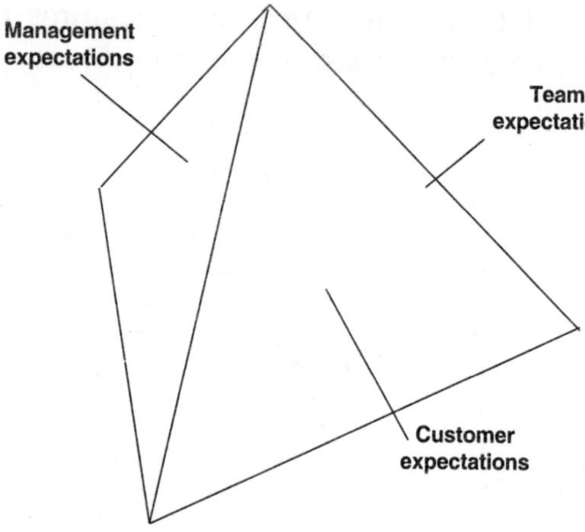

Figure 2: Triple Expectations Pyramid

Instead of a simple triangle, prefer a Triple Expectations Pyramid (Figure 2). As shown, each face of the pyramid concerns the expectations of one of the following: your customer, your management, or your team. Each face of the pyramid is itself also a triple constraint triangle, with schedule, cost, and performance (requirement or scope) constraints. Successfully balancing these nine constraints simultaneously is what provides the environment within which a project manager can succeed.

Success is not simply meeting the technical goals—that is, the schedule, cost, and performance goals that were given out early in the project. Leaders doggedly do so and yet subsequently fail to thrive in their careers. This is because they do not balance the expectations of their customers, their management, and their teams with the technical goals of the project.

More powerful is the leader who may not meet all the technical requirements but still somehow thrives. Often people ascribe this success to politics or to connections. Sometimes this is true, but often something more profound has occurred. Expectations are often unspoken and possibly not fully understood even by the person with the expectations. Possessors of high emotional intelligence have a leg up on the rest of us here.

Project leaders who develop high emotional intelligence are better able to simultaneously balance the technical requirements and these key stakeholder expectations in a way that satisfies all involved. Develop is the key word in the preceding sentence; turns out there is hope for all of us. This is because, unlike IQ, which seems to be fairly constant throughout one's lifetime, EQ can be learned. Many executive business coaches focus heavily on EQ with their clients, often to good effect.

After all, successful leaders care about what customers and project team members think, so it is natural that project leaders who can incorporate the expectations of these groups into their overall project solution will be valued. Think of the sports world, another area of intense pressure where high performance is rewarded and poor performance is visibly punished.

Great coaches in the sports world also successfully create winning teams in chaotic, dynamic environments with a set of diverse stakeholders they don't control. It makes sense that a leader is better appreciated if the leader can include the often-unstated expectations of these stakeholders in the final approach. Succeeding within the Expectations Pyramid is defined as being able to balance schedule, cost, and performance goals simultaneously with the expectations of your customer, management, and team so that all parties are satisfied with the results.

Grace, a project manager in a well-known technology company, was promoted to VP after she was able to master the Expectations Pyramid on a project that was very important to her corporation and to the survival of the design center in which the project was located.

Grace took over a design centre that had failed quite publicly on a previous project and was possibly in danger of being closed. Grace was able to leverage this expectation of closure into a huge personal commitment from the team. She also, for the most part, protected her design center—quite remote from the corporation's Silicon Valley headquarters—from management's addition of desired functionality (scope creep) through a single-minded intensity and focus that convinced all parties that she would succeed.

Expectations of Your Customer

The customer expects the product to be delivered for the lowest cost and on schedule, with the features she was promised and/or visualises. She is concerned that her money is being wasted and that the project is not getting the best and the brightest or the right focus within your organization. She worries that you and your management food chain aren't telling the truth. Her actions are driven by these worries and concerns, by her expectations about her fears.

Several statements from project managers highlight the disconnect between customer expectations for performance and the team's desire to do creative work that comes from customer expectations.

These pain points often result in a lot of extra work for everyone involved. I'm sure you have additional pain point examples of your own. Pain points that come from the customer include:

- He has unrealistic dates.
- She tells team what to do. How can drive the team when the customer is directing them?
- He backstabs with management.
- She is always pushing for more features and doesn't want a cost or schedule impact.

As a project manager, you have to ask yourself why the customer undertakes these actions. The answer is not as simple as "People are illogical." Actually, they aren't illogical. They are almost always very logical, if only you take the time to find out the basis of their logic. If you don't understand why the customer is acting this way, your chances of successfully satisfying that customer will drop, and a great deal of your precious time may be wasted while you try to deal with the ramifications of that lack of knowledge. Let's look at each pain point from a viewpoint that includes the customer's motivations.

- He has unrealistic dates. Does he have unrealistic dates because he believes your company sandbagged the schedule or because of a toxic management style in which he pressures you for an aggressive date to ensure that you will make your more conservative date?
- She tells team what to do. How can drive the team when the customer is directing them? Does she tells your team what to do simply because you let

her do so? Or does she think you don't know what you're doing and she has to direct the team for you to ensure her success? Does she do so because of an "I'm paying for this" mentality?

- He backstabs with management. Does your customer do this in an effort to leverage extra things from your management? Or is he simply just talking with an old friend (your boss) in an effort to ensure success?
- She is always pushing for more features and doesn't want a cost or schedule impact. Customers always want more, and often they don't know what they really want when the project starts. You have to determine if the customer is pushing for more in an effort to get something for free or because she is puzzling it out as she goes.

To succeed, you must understand the answers to these questions and come up with solutions that work for everyone. To do so, apply your key set of values, if communication and trust are key values, then explain to the customer that you would like that sort of relationship. Also, throughout the project, use your values as a way to politely question the customer on his or her actions. In this way, you will gain congruence with your customer through your values.

Expectations of Your Management

Your management food chain expects to build future business with the customer; hence, it will, from your point of view, tend to appease the customer. Your project is likely only one aspect of your organization's relationship with the customer. Your supervisor expects sales and profit growth in his business area. He is concerned that the customer can't be pleased and that he may be unable—due to time or other constraints—to ensure the success of the project. He is worried that he can't trust you to protect him and the organization. These types of worries and concerns drive his subsequent actions.

Here are some of the pain points involving supervisors or management that are commonly mentioned by project managers. Let's look at each pain point from a view that includes possible management motivations.

- *He micromanages me.* Maybe your supervisor is just trying to be extra-precise in his efforts to help you. Maybe he doesn't trust you, or perhaps just the contrary, and what you view as micromanagement is simply an overreaction to being ignored by his prior management.
- *She manages upward; she ignores me.* Maybe she has poor people skills and simply doesn't know how to properly mentor or coach you. Perhaps she is truly evil and cares only for herself. Or perhaps she has the sort of personality that prefers to serve those above her rather than leading those below.
- *He wants me not to tell the customer (or upper management) the truth.* Is he being micromanaged? Has a customer in his past who knew too many details about how the sausage was made caused him pain?
- *She wants to know all the minute details.* Does she act this way because she lacks trust, or does she act this way because she was trained to expect that technical managers should know everything that is going on in their organizations? Perhaps she is simply not able to realize that different levels of an organization require different management skill sets.

Why do they act this way?; ask yourself as you ponder these statements and others like them. Then you must find a solution that will work for you.

Expectations of Your Team

The team expects to do cool, interesting, cutting-edge work. Individual team members worry that project management (you) will give in to customer and management demands that will lessen the team's creativity and, ultimately, their fun. Their actions are driven by these worries, and thus they may tend to do what they prefer rather than what they are told to do, especially if there is no perceived personal penalty for doing so. This makes it particularly important that project managers learn how to inclusively manage and to be able to uncover team member concerns and incorporate them into appropriate solutions.

Some common team pain points are listed here. Let's look at each pain point from a view that includes possible motivations for your team.

- I'm a manager; they don't respect me. Are you still trying to be one of the gang? Are you still trying to be a technical expert at one or more of the areas of expertise on your team? Do you fill the proper role of a project manager to lead the team?
- They ignore direction. Perhaps your direction is misguided or even wrong. Consider whether your guidance helps team members solve their problems.
- They complain and whine constantly. Why can't they just work? Are they bad people you should get rid of? That's pretty difficult. Or maybe you just haven't listened to and helped them with their real issues.
- They hide the truth. This means they don't trust you. Figure out how to win their trust. The best suggestion have for you is to quit looking at the project from your perspective and instead to look at

it from your team's viewpoint. Do that, and trust will blossom.

Again, answer for yourself why your team of outstanding people is doing these things. What do their actions have to do with your actions or inactions? What values are you managing them to? What can you do about all this?

❖❖❖

SELECTED READINGS

Albert Hamilton. *Handbook of Project Management Procedures*. TTL Publishing, Ltd. 2003.

Bjarne Kousholt. *Project Management: Theory and practice*. Nyt Teknisk Forlag. 2007.

Bossidy, Larry, and Ram Charan. *Execution: The Discipline of Getting Things Done*. New York: Crown Business, 2002.

Collins, Jim. *Good to Great: Why Some Companies Make the Leap... and Others Don't*. New York: HarperCollins, 2001.

Connors, Roger, and Tom Smith. *How Did That Happen?: Holding People Accountable for Results the Positive, Principled Way*. New York: Portfolio, 2009.

Covey, Stephen P. *The 8th Habit: From Effectiveness to Greatness*. New York: Free Press, 2004.

David I. Cleland, Roland Gareis. *Global project management handbook*. McGraw-Hill Professional, 2006.

Davis, David. "Beware of False Economies." *Harvard Business Review on Managing Projects*. Boston: Harvard Business School Press, 2005.

Dennis Lock. *Project management*. Gower Publishing, Ltd., 2007.

Fleming, Quentin W., and Joel M. Hoppelman. *Earned Value Project Management*. Newton Square, Penn.: Project Management Institute, 1996.

Harold Kerzner. *Project Management: A Systems Approach to Planning, Scheduling, and Controlling*. Wiley. 2003.

Harrison, F. L. Dennis Lock. *Advanced project management: a structured approach*?. Gower Publishing, Ltd., 2004.

Hesselbein, Frances. Hesselbein on Leadership. San Francisco: Jossey-Bass, 2002. Highsmith, Jim. *Agile Project Management: Creating Innovative Products*. Boston: Addison-Wesley, 2004.

Jörg Becker, Martin Kugeler, Michael Rosemann. *Process management: a guide for the design of business processes.* 2003

Joseph Phillips. *PMP Project Management Professional Study Guide.* McGraw-Hill Professional, 2003.

Kendrick, Tom. *Results without Authority: Controlling a Project When the Team Doesn't Report to You.* New York: AMACOM, 2006.

Kerzner, Harold. *Project Management: A Systems Approach to Planning, Scheduling, and Controlling.* 6th ed. New York: Wiley, 1998.

Krzyzewski, Mike. *The Gold Standard: Building a World-Class Team.* With Jamie K. Spatola. New York: Business Plus, 2009.

Lewis R. Ireland. *Project Management.* McGraw-Hill Professional, 2006.

Martin Stevens. *Project Management Pathways. Association for Project Management.* APM Publishing Limited, 2002.

Matta, Nadim F., and Ronald N. Ashkenas. "Why Good Projects Fail Anyway." *Harvard Business Review on Managing Projects.* Boston: Harvard Business School Press, 2005.

McFarland, Grant. *Microprocessor Design: A Practical Guide from Design Planning to Manufacturing.* New York: McGraw-Hill, 2006.

Mersino, Anthony C. *Emotional Intelligence for Project Managers: The People Skills You Need to Achieve Outstanding Results.* New York: AMACOM, 2007.

Paul C. Dinsmore et al. *The right projects done right*! John Wiley and Sons, 2005.

Warner Books, 1992. Project Management Institute. *A Guide to the Project Management Body of Knowledge: PMBOK Guide.* 3rd ed. Newton Square, Penn: Project Management Institute, 2004.

Young-Hoon Kwak. "A brief history of Project Management". In: *The story of managing projects.* Elias G. Carayannis et al. (9 eds), Greenwood Publishing Group, 2005.